KENFIG FOLK ...

# THE FIRST BOROUGH
# OF
# KENFIG
## *1147 – 1439*

*Barrie Griffiths*

**THE KENFIG SOCIETY**

*Published in the UK by the Kenfig Society*
*3 Cwm Cadno, Margam, Wales SA13 2TP, UK*

Registered Charity no. 702279

Website: www.kenfigsociety.org

ISBN: **978-0-9567701-0-3**

A CIP catalogue record for this book is available from the British Library
Printed by ImprintDigital.net, Exeter EX5 5HY, UK

## Barrie Griffiths 1942 – 2009

Barrie was that best of amateur historians — enthusiastic, knowledgeable yet sceptical about what he read and saw. As a retired police-sergeant it came naturally to him to question the evidence, especially the earlier writings of those prone to mystic fantasy. Nor would Barrie accept the confident assertions of 'experts'; only by weighing the evidence would he come to a conclusion.

In this series of books Barrie lays out the depth of his knowledge and understanding of Kenfig over a period of 700 years, from the coming of the Anglo-Normans to the mid-Victorian era. Barrie, a colourful character in life, wanted to explain Kenfig and its story, but also what was going on in the wider world and how it affected the town. He does this in his own inimitable style, and has produced a highly readable account, which should please both the general reader and the historical specialist alike.

Never one to shrink from controversy, after 20 years or more of close examination and reflection on the evidence, Barrie was able to form many new insights and interpretations, which will be found in these pages. But this is not done in a rancorous way — reasonableness and good humour shine out from Barrie's account of the life of Kenfig Folk.

**Note from the editing committee:**

We have retained Barrie's text in full, only changing a few details of the layout. Some of the titles have been altered to make the subject clearer. Originally Barrie had included many photographs to show the area. A problem is that one picture of the dunes with a bit of old castle sticking up looks like any other! So there are fewer pictures, intended solely to illustrate a point that Barrie was making. Thanks are due to Cyril James for re-photographing many of them, as well as some new views. Thanks to John Ball for the photo of the drawing of Kenfig in 1805 and Google-earth for the aerial picture of The Angel Inn, Mawdlam.

Of course any changes would normally be checked and approved by the author. Instead we formed an editing committee consisting of Terry Robbins, Ken Williams, Brian James, Keith & Janis Edger and Dennis Jones. But as the person in overall charge mine is the final responsibility for any errors or omissions.

Conall Boyle,
Publications Secretary,
Kenfig Society

April 2011


*The front cover shows the remains of Kenfig Castle. Photo by Cyril James.*

# KENFIG FOLK

## An Introduction to the Series

At the time of writing I have spent over 20 years researching the story of Kenfig, gathering information as and when I find it. It would also be true to say that there is still a considerable body of material that I have yet to explore, but there comes a time when the local historian has to bite the bullet and start getting the results of his labours together and put them down on paper! Knowledge that is not recorded is knowledge that is lost. At this point some awkward choices have to be faced.

Twenty years work has produced a heck of a lot of material, and rightly or wrongly I chose to write it in the form of a book, albeit one that I knew at the outset would never be published [in Barrie's lifetime. Ed.]. I have divided my story of the *Kenfig Folk* into five parts. The first part *The First Borough of Kenfig 1147-1439*, covers the story of the settlement adjoining the castle from the time of its founding in the middle of the 12th century to its abandonment nearly three centuries later. In this I am following in the footsteps of Thomas Gray (1909, *The Buried City of Kenfig)* and A. Leslie Evans (1964, *The Story of Kenfig*). In the main I have tried to avoid merely re-hashing what they have written and concentrated instead on placing the town and its inhabitants in the context of the history of the surrounding area: Why it was attacked so often by the Welsh? How did the people there manage to make their living? I have also looked at the question of how, why and when the town was eventually abandoned, and hopefully made an important contribution to Kenfig's history in this area.

Part II, *The Borough in the Sands* will continue the story of the Borough into the Tudor Period and onwards to the year 1699. Here I have tried to look at its history through the eyes of the people who lived there, and to follow the lives of certain individuals and families to whom Kenfig was 'home'. We also follow their battle to keep the Borough organisation in being, and to amend and adapt its institutions to meet the altered circumstances of its situation. Their battle against the sand encroachment that had claimed their medieval town and castle was far from over, and more fields, buildings, and even a small hamlet were lost during these years. Then there were the religious changes spawned by Henry VIII's break with Rome which split our tiny community to its core with rival groups of Catholics, Nonconformists and Anglicans. Amongst all this upheaval and change, a living still had to be made and children fed. Hopefully I have managed to capture the essence of this in what I have written.

The third part, *Recession, Famine and Bussy Mansel*, covers a period of just half a century between 1700 and 1750. This was however a crucial period in the Borough's history that subsequently forced changes to be made in its organisation. It was also a time when the population itself was in flux. Some families stood their ground and rode out the storm, but many either died out or left the area to seek a new life elsewhere. They in their turn were replaced by others, some of whom stayed only for a short time before moving on. It was a time when the economy of Kenfig and the surrounding areas collapsed, disease and famine made inroads into the population, and the Margam estate—which was the major landowner in the Borough—was brought to its knees.

Part IV, *Twilight of the Portreeves* follows the Borough's history from 1750 to the end of the century. It was a time when outsiders began visiting Kenfig and leaving some record of the community they saw. It also looks in some depth at the allegation that the people here were 'wreckers' – deliberately luring ships onto Sker Point in order to plunder their cargoes. In this context particular attention is paid to the wreck of the sloop *Caterina* in 1781 for which there is a particularly large body of documentary material available. Most importantly perhaps it also looks at the changes apparent in the organisation of the Borough itself altering, and in some ways, weakening the system that had served the burgesses so well since their abandonment of their former medieval town.

As its title suggests, Part V, *Fading into the Future* follows the gradual disintegration of the Borough as it became an increasingly irrelevant organisation in the rapidly burgeoning world of industrialised Britain. It cover the first fifty years of the 19th century and ends with an overview of the Lower Borough of Kenfig in the year 1850 based largely upon the census returns of 1841 and 1851, and the tithe map of 1846. At this point my current research ends and at this point in time I have no intention of taking it any further forward towards the 20th century. There is more than enough unread material relating to the years I have already covered to keep me occupied for many years to come yet!

I still, for example, have to make a proper survey of the Margam Parish Registers for the details of the burgesses from Higher Kenfig, just one of a host of 'small jobs' waiting to be done that will dot the I's and cross the T's in my current history. At the same time there are literally scores of documents relating to Kenfig that I am aware exist, but have yet to read. What follows therefore is a history based on what I know now. Hopefully I will gradually be able to expand and improve it in the years that follow.

Before I close these notes however, there are two people in particular that have assisted me along the way and who deserve a special mention. Mrs Jean Evans of Llandow near Cowbridge, and Mr Dennis Jones of North Cornelly have spent considerable time and effort proof-reading each section of this history as it has been completed. Whilst hereby putting on record my sincere and heartfelt thanks for their suggestions, corrections and encouragement. Let me say too that any errors that remain are mine, and mine alone!

Barrie, October, 2008

Kenfig Folk: Part I

# THE FIRST BOROUGH
# OF
# KENFIG
## *1147 – 1439*

*Barrie Griffiths*

# Contents

# Maps

# INTRODUCTION TO PART 1:

That I ever got involved in a study of the medieval Borough of Kenfig is down to the late Rennie Davies. When the Kenfig Society first formed in February 1989 I had just completed a ten year project on the history of the manors of Stormy and Horgrove[1] and it was the creation of this new organisation that suggested to me where my next venture should be. Not that I intended bothering too much with the glories of Kenfig's medieval past—far from it! It was the story of the earliest Norman settlements that had first attracted me to Stormy, but from that I had gone on to trace what I felt was the equally fascinating (if not so dramatic) tale of the area during the two centuries after 1650.

The earlier history of Kenfig had been well covered by local historians Thomas Gray (*The Buried City of Kenfig*, 1909) and A. Leslie Evans (*The Kenfig Story*, 1964), so there seemed little point in re-hashing what they had already written. Instead my intention was to utilise the new knowledge I had gained at Stormy to take the story of the Borough on from the destruction of the town to its eventual abolition in 1886. In itself this promised to be an ambitious enough project so I had no intention of wasting valuable time on the earlier history. That good intention however did not long survive Rennie's appointment as the Society's first Co-ordinator[2] for our archaeological excavation.

Already during the brief span of the Society's existence the two of us had enjoyed discussing and arguing about various aspects of the early history of the medieval town. With the start of 'the dig'

---

[1] *Sturmi's Land* (1990). Unpublished MSS available at Bridgend County Libraries

[2] The Society has never actually got round to giving the person 'in charge' of the excavation a formal title! Dennis Jones who holds this post at the time of writing prefers the title of 'Co-ordinator' and, to my mind it best describes his role which involves not only determining the actual course of operations but also the involvement of other bodies such as archaeologists, conservators and museums

now looming, he asked me if I would produce something bringing together what was known about its medieval history. This involved not just collating the information available but also looking more closely at several theories about it that had been advanced in recent years, and then producing a kind of 'hand-book' against which the archaeologists could measure any discoveries they made on the ground. At the time I was not too excited by the project but Rennie insisted, and I'm glad he did.

If we go back to the mid 1950s when I first began to get interested in local history there were some obvious and glaring gaps in the story of Kenfig's past. The Victorian era had produced a body of solid and dependable (and often unreadable!) material from the likes of Clark, Birch, Corbet and Gray but, except for the last named, none offered much in the way of explanation as to either Kenfig's origin or its eventual demise. Gray, it is true, carried the story of Kenfig back to the days of the Vikings, but based this on material supplied by the notorious historical forger Iolo Morgannwg which therefore made it highly suspect to say the least!

What can be said with certainty is that a number of stray finds from the Roman period have come to light in the vicinity over the years, and (although a theory not currently in vogue) local place names seem to indicate a Norse or Danish settlement somewhere in the vicinity. At the present time the location of this still awaits discovery and may, or may not prove that it was situated at the site where the Norman town was built in the 12th century

The same is true of the end of the medieval town some centuries later. Clearly it had been eventually overwhelmed by sand, but how, why, and (perhaps most importantly) when, nobody seemed to know. The great achievement of these solid Victorians was the collection, cataloguing and publication of such documents that survived from the medieval period, but anything not included in these was largely passed over in silence.

It is only during the last half century that things have begun to change and historians, amateur and professional, are reevaluating the material so painstakingly collected by our predecessors to build upon the work they had done. Some theories offered about Kenfig's past have much to commend them; others are dubious; and some are plainly absurd. This history of mine falls into this body of research, though I leave for others to judge which category it merits!

The typescript I eventually handed over to Rennie was in the form of a narrative history of medieval Kenfig, copies of which were also placed in the local library. To assist me, I also drew upon some earlier research I had carried out utilising Birch's *Margam Abbey* (1897) in which I had attempted to assign approximate dates to the Margam MSS dating from the 12th and early 13th centuries. The method I used seemed to achieve a certain success, and is set out in Appendix VI. The document I produced for the Society was not, nor was it intended to be, a particularly readable account of Kenfig's history, but this was subsequently attempted in the form of five booklets entitled *Medieval Kenfig* published between 1996 to 1998.

My current version draws heavily upon the information contained in these, but is aimed principally at the general reader who has but little interest in the evolution of theories about the past. Moreover I also wanted to tackle the history of the Borough from a slightly difficult angle. The known facts about medieval Kenfig have been published by Gray and Evans, so there was little point in a history that merely repeats what they have said in a different form. Instead I have tried to produce a document that looks in greater detail at what the records tell us about the town's history and development. Why, for example, did it become such a focus for Welsh resentment? How did it survive despite being the target of at least nine attacks upon it in less than two centuries? Most important of all perhaps—how, why and when, having survived these repeated attempts to obliterate it, was it subsequently abandoned?

In the main therefore it is these questions that my own history of Kenfig seeks to address, uncovering the story behind the bare bones provided by contemporary records.

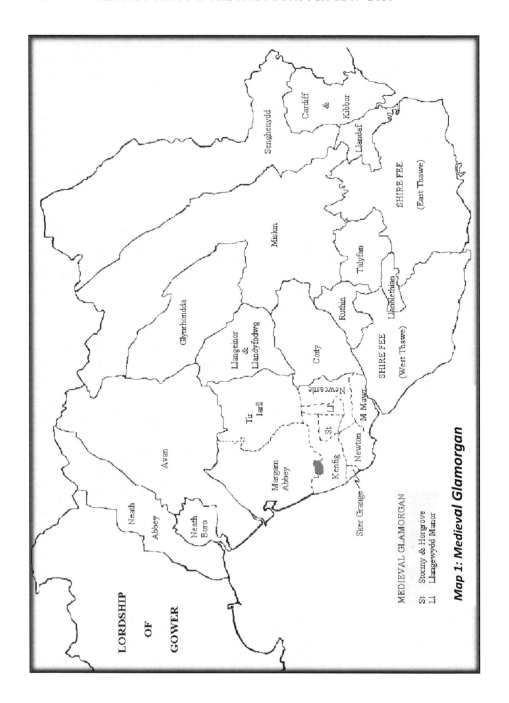

Map 1: *Medieval Glamorgan*

# Chapter 1

## THE ANGLO-NORMAN CONQUEST

Although Robert FitzHamon has received the credit for being the Norman conqueror of the land that subsequently became the Lordship of Glamorgan, it has become quite clear that his conquest was not as complete as was once believed. Indeed, if we are to be strictly correct all he actually did was to establish a Norman presence within the former Welsh kingdom from which the eventual 'conquest' followed piecemeal over succeeding centuries, and only after bitter fighting.

On the open land of the Glamorgan Vale the lightly-armed Welshmen had little chance against FitzHamon's small but heavily armoured force of mounted knights. But in the wooded hills and foothills of the Blaenau the effectiveness of the latter were nullified by the terrain. Whether the Elizabethan historian Rice Merrick (Merrick, 1578: 30-2) was quoting from oral tradition passed down through the Glamorgan bardic circle, or just giving his own interpretation of the situation we cannot tell. Nevertheless the sequence of events that he describes following the initial invasion is one that few modern historians would now quarrel with.

Driven from the coastal plain, the Welsh regrouped "in the lower mountains, in the frontiers of the low country [and] with often [in]roads and incursions assailed the strangers, sometimes out of one part of the mountains, sometimes out of another". This, Merrick tells us was in order to obtain the wherewithal to survive for, as he explains, "the mountains in those days bore no such corn as now groweth thereon".

Peace terms were, he claims, offered and rejected, so FitzHamon

> considering with how small resistance he had gotten the low country …. determined to force them either simply to yield or to persecute them with sharp war and so conquer the rest.

His attempts to invade the Blaenau were a disaster:

> The Welshmen, not able for want of artillery to encounter with them in plain field, taking them in places of advantage, either ascending or descending from on high and steep hills, so courageously set upon them that they were often put to flights, and divers places made notorious by their slaughter.

**Robert FitzHamon & his wife.shown holding a model of Tewkesbury Abbey**
*(from a 17th Century Manuscript)*

It is clear to us today that the Normans indeed failed to effect a permanent foothold in the hill territory and consequently (to again quote Merrick) they "determined strongly to fence the frontiers of the low country next toward the mountains" with castles. These were situated at locations where they would discourage raids on the land further south and also, as Merrick suggests, force the Welsh to sue for terms because of the lack of food resources in the hill country.

The ruins of many of these castles are still with us today if one knows where to look. Forget your visions of crumbling towers and walls, these were small strongholds of earth and timber that have largely decayed back into the soil from which they were born so as to be all but invisible to the untrained eye. But they are there nevertheless—a whole necklace of them lies strung along the A48 highway between Culverhouse Cross (in Cardiff) and Cowbridge, now nothing more than overgrown mounds and weed-filled ditches. Keeping Cardiff and some of the best land in the Vale for himself, FitzHamon parcelled out the remainder amongst his followers as manors for which they owed him 'knight's service' in the form of 'castle guard'. This involved providing the services of a knight and his retainers to perform guard duty at Cardiff Castle for a specified number of days per year. The lord of a manor was rated at 'one knight's fee' and had to perform the service for 40 days; half a fee meant 20 days; whilst two knight's fees could be served by two knights for 40 days or one carrying out the duty for double that period. In due course it was replaced by a fixed payment known as 'wardsilver'. These lands held by such service became known as the 'Shire Fee'. For the purposes of administration the shire of Glamorgan was divided into East and West Thaw[3].

There were three knights however, who were treated as special cases and held their land on purely nominal terms. These were the so-called 'member lordships' of Glamorgan. It has been suggested that their owners secured them through acting independently of the main Norman invasion. On this point I have my doubts, for certainly all three original lordships were situated at key points within Glamorgan which in the medieval period stretched no further west than the Crymlyn Brook at Jersey Marine. Swansea and the Gower were only added to form the County of Glamorgan under the Act of Union of England and Wales in the time of King Henry VIII.

Cowbridge, at the very heart of the Vale, had been a prosperous little town on the main highway through South Wales in the days of the Romans. It now seems clear however that once they departed the site was abandoned and nothing existed here until a

---

[3] This is the river Thaw which meets the Bristol Channel at Aberthaw.(ed.)

borough town was built in the middle of the 13th century. It lay within the boundary of a member lordship held by one of the De St Quentin family whose main base was at Llanblethian a little further down the valley of the Thaw. This is apparently because at that time it was here, and not Cowbridge[4], that the main highway from Cardiff crossed the river. The St Quentins controlled the ford by building a castle on the eastern side and another facing it across the valley at Caer Dynnaf[5]. Further evidence of the pre-eminence of Llanblethian during the early stages of Norman settlement is the fact that it is the church there that was, and still is, the parish church for Cowbridge. The town's own church is rated as merely a 'chapel of ease'.

**Llanblethian Castle from the South-East.**
*(from a 1741 engraving by Buck)*

---

[4] There is, in fact, no reference to a settlement at Cowbridge in any documents relating to Glamorgan until the middle of the 13th century. Archaeologists I have spoken with who have been involved in excavations at Cowbridge likewise confirm that they found no evidence of any re-occupation following the abandonment of the Roman settlement until this period.
[5] Though not visible today, a castle is mentioned at this location by Merrick, and some ruins are indicated in this location in an engraving of Quentin's castle (which is the one on the eastern side of the valley) by Samuel and Nathaniel Buck circa 1740.

Coity, north of Bridgend, the home of the Turberville family was another such 'member lordship' and occupied a triangular peninsula of land between the rivers Ewenny and Ogmore almost to their confluence near Ogmore Castle. Legend has it that the first Turberville—a man known as Payne or Pagan—secured this land through his own efforts by a mixture of force and diplomacy involving marriage to a Welsh heiress. To understand its strategic importance to the Norman settlement, however, one has to picture the area as it was in his day. At that time the Ewenny River was flanked by marshes (the legacy of a former glacial lake) from Pencoed right down to Ewenny bridge (Randall, 1962: 20), creating an effective barrier to travellers along those reaches. A little below the crossing a smaller area of low-lying marshy ground (often flooded during the winter even today) continues down to Ogmore Castle.

The bridge at Ewenny therefore marks the site of a crossing that has probably been in use since Roman times and their road presumably headed directly west from here. As at Cowbridge however it had been abandoned and all trace of its former course lost by the time of the Norman invasion. The highway used by the newcomers therefore headed northwards from Ewenny through the Turberville land and crossed the Ogmore River at what is now Bridgend. Here the Turbervilles built a fortress (later known as Oldcastle) below the rocky bluff overlooking this stretch of river. Further north much of the land within their lordship was heavily wooded[6]. Their main fortress at Coity stood at the heart of this forest with tracks leading off in all directions[7] and thereby dominating

---

[6] Memories of this forest linger not only in the name Coity (Coed Ty or Coed Du), but elsewhere throughout the surrounding district, e.g. Pencoed, Coed y Mwstwr, and Coychurch (Coed Church).

[7] My description of the Norman frontier on the lower Ogmore River largely follows research by H. J. Randall set out in his 1953 book *Bridgend – The Story of a Market Town*. He, however, was sceptical about there ever having been a fortress at Oldcastle for which there is, in fact, quite convincing evidence. This is set out in the *Inventory of Ancient Monuments*

local communications and the approaches to the southern portion of their lordship in a manner that is not immediately apparent today.

As is believed to have been the case at Llanblethian, the key crossing of the river Ogmore at Bridgend was guarded by two castles—the Turberville's Oldcastle on one side being matched by FitzHamon's own fortress at Newcastle on the other. Having crossed the river the road ascended Newcastle hill and then in the shadow of the castle turned west to Laleston[8].

The defence of the lower Ogmore river was completed by the De Londres fortress at Ogmore which guarded the tidal fords on the lower reaches of both this river and the Ewenny. Finally, in 1141, the system was completed by the construction of the priory at Ewenny, though whether it was fortified at this early stage we do not know.

Beyond the walls of Newcastle and Ogmore the territory to the west was debatable land still dominated in the early 12th century by the Welsh. [See Map 1 on p. 16]. I have a theory (and it is no more than this) that at an early stage in the Norman invasion they pushed through this area and the narrow gap between the coast and the hills where Port Talbot now stands to take possession of land further west. Certainly they obtained a foothold on the west bank of the river Neath where a castle was built somewhere in the vicinity of the later abbey. This was a dangerous and exposed outpost which during outbreaks of hostilities with the Welsh was often cut off from overland contact with the main Norman base in the Vale. Yet it was vital that it remained as tangible proof of FitzHamon's claim to hold all Glamorgan up to the Crymlyn Brook and thereby prevent encroachment by his Norman neighbours in Swansea and the

---

*in Glamorgan, Volume III, Part 1a, The Early Castles* published by The Royal Commission on Ancient & Historical Monuments in Wales, 1991, pp 159-60.

[8] The main street of this village is described as the "highway from Cardiff to Kenfig" in a late 12th century grant of some adjoining land by Thomas de Lageles (*Penrice&Margam* 292.13). This probably remained the course of the main road until the mid 13th century when the crossing of the Ogmore at New Inn Bridge ('The Dipping Bridge') was created.

*Defence along the Ogmore river.*
*Ogmore Castle (above)*
*(below) EwennyPriory, the monastery built like a castle*

Gower. Here therefore was the third 'member lordship' which was entrusted to a certain Richard de Granville.

It is also part of my theory that as part of this Norman thrust towards the west, castles were established not just at Newcastle and Neath Abbey but possibly at Kenfig and Aberafan as well. These would have secured a line of communication for the invasion force to their base in the Vale of Glamorgan. When the Welsh of South Wales launched a counter-offensive in 1095 these two were probably abandoned with Aberafan being re-occupied by the Welsh.

FitzHamon died in 1107 leaving a daughter named Matilda as sole heiress to his lands in England and Wales and, as was the custom under feudal law, she became a ward of the King who at this time was Henry I. It therefore being his responsibility to choose her a husband he selected, from among his many illegitimate offspring, one known as Robert of Caen (subsequently created Earl of Gloucester) who now took control of her estates.

As Merrick (1578) says, it was this Robert who brought about an end at last to the perpetual hostilities between the invaders and the native population in Glamorgan. Again there seems to be an element of truth in what he says: in 1141 during the civil war with King Stephen, for example, Robert brought an army of Welsh troops raised on his estates onto the battlefield at Lincoln. It was during this period too that certain Welsh chieftains emerge as 'member lords' of lands in the unconquered hill territory.

The most important of these from our point of view was a Caradoc ap Iestyn. He was claimed to have been the eldest son of the last native ruler of Glamorgan. He held sway over all the hill country between the rivers Neath and Taff and we assume that he and the other lesser native lords were allowed to hold these lands through some kind of accommodation with the Normans.

The period of the Earl's rule at this time was not a tranquil one: there were certainly several eruptions of violence during the 1120s. It has been suggested, for example, that a hoard of coins discovered during excavations of a ring-work castle at Llantrithyd was deposited in 1122-4 in circumstances that indicate violent destruction of the building[9]. In 1127 the Annals of Margam Abbey (Davies, 2003: 46) tell us that Caradoc and his brothers slew a certain Roger Ymor and "as well as being perjured towards him they committed sacrilege, breaking into two churches, namely Saint Tydog's and Saint Tathan's".

Saint Tydog's is presumably the one at Tythegston which in later times was part of the manor of Newcastle. This brief reference therefore perhaps relates to a raid carried out by Caradoc to consolidate his position west of the Ogmore frontier and then continued onwards into the lands of the Vale. At about the same time Richard de Granville was finding his exposed position at Neath becoming increasingly untenable as Rice Merrick discovered from the Register of Neath Abbey[10].

From his information (Merrick, 1578: 53-4) it seems quite clear that in 1129 Granville, having founded the Abbey at Neath at the request of his dying wife Constance, turned all his land west of the river over to the monks and left for a quieter life on his estates in the West Country. Evidence of the circumstances of his departure is contained in two further grants of land instanced by Merrick. These were in favour of two of Caradoc's brothers named Rhys and Rhiwallon and were made "pro bono pacis" (for a lasting peace) prior to 1129.

The hostilities that brought this about also seem to have led to the creation of the town and castle of Neath on the opposite bank of the river. Granville was the constable of the latter prior to his departure. The land on which the Borough of Neath is situated is on the eastern side of the river, and logically one would have expected this to be part and parcel of the Welsh lordship of Avan. It has in fact the appearance of being carved out of Avan, and may therefore have been seized from Caradoc by Earl Robert during the course of

---

[9] *Morgannwg*, Vol VI (1962), pp 100-1

[10] To the infinite regret of modern historians this document has unfortunately long since vanished.

these hostilities during the 1120s. With De Granville increasingly reluctant to remain in his exposed outpost the creation of a fortified settlement here retained a Norman presence on his western boundary.

The Earl was soon engulfed by far greater and more pressing problems than such purely domestic issues however. Following the death of his sons in the wreck of the *White Ship,* King Henry's only legitimate surviving child was a daughter named Matilda, generally known as 'The Empress Matilda' from a former marriage to The Holy Roman Emperor. Desperate to ensure her succession to the throne, the King had the leading barons of his Kingdom swear fealty to her twice in his own lifetime, but it seems most of them must have kept their fingers crossed when they did so! They neither fancied being ruled by a woman nor allowing her new husband, Geoffrey of Anjou, to have any authority over them. Consequently as soon as Henry was safely dead they invited his nephew, Stephen of Blois, to be their ruler. He was duly crowned as King Stephen at Westminster Abbey in 1135.

One person who had no intention of accepting this state of affairs was the Empress herself, and finding support amongst certain factions within the Anglo-Norman nobility, she attempted to oust the usurper by force. This was the start of a long and bloody civil war in which neither side ever succeeded in achieving outright victory. When it broke out Earl Robert found himself in an interesting position. He was of royal blood and his illegitimacy was not of itself necessarily a bar to his advancing his own claim to the succession. After all, the mother of his grand-sire, William The Conqueror, had been the daughter of a tanner.

In the event Earl Robert gave unstinting support to his half sister, and his loyalty to her never wavered for the remainder of his life. Indirectly, however, his involvement in the Civil War may well have led to the foundation of the Borough of Kenfig, and this now brings us to the story of Owain's greyhound.

This story is recorded by the cleric Giraldus Cambrensis who travelled through Wales in 1188 in the train of Baldwin the Archbishop of Canterbury. They were here to 'preach the crusade' – raising a volunteer army to save Jerusalem from the invading Saracens. Whilst on his travels Giraldus kept an account of the country, its people, and the various stories he heard along the way. The tale of Owain's greyhound is one of a number he was told when the Archbishop's party stayed overnight at Margam Abbey. The credit for realising its significance belongs to Prof J. Beverley Smith (Smith, 1958: 9-17) though at about the same time the late Leslie Evans, working independently, also advanced a similar hypothesis in an unpublished manuscript which I believe was called *Leyson D'Avene* (Evans, n/k). In the words of Giraldus the story he heard went as follows:

> It also happened in our own lifetime, when the four sons of Caradog ap Iestin ... were ruling in their father's stead over the lands which they were eventually to inherit (as is the custom among the Welsh) that, in a fit of jealousy and malice ...Cadwallon murdered his brother Owain. The wrath of God soon caught up with him. He was leading an assault on a certain castle when a wall collapsed on top of him and he was crushed to pieces and killed. In the presence of many of his own and his brothers' troops he died a miserable death and so paid the penalty which he deserved This same Owain had a greyhound which was very tall and handsome, its coat being streaked with a variety of colours. It defended its master and in so doing was wounded in seven places, for it was shot through the body with arrows and prodded with spears. In return it bit and tore at Owain's assailants and those who were assassinating him. Its wounds healed, but they left scars. Later the dog was sent by William, Earl of Gloucester to Henry II ...as evidence of this remarkable achievement. (Giraldus, 1987: 128).

The sons of Caradoc are named as Morgan, Maredudd, Owain and Cadwallon, and of these we know that Morgan, Maredudd and Cadwallon subsequently ruled over the Welsh member lordships of Avan, Miskin and Glynrhondda respectively. In his interpretation of the Giraldus' account Prof Smith states that the monks had said that Owain held land 'hereabouts' implying the district in which their monastery stood.

As documents that survive from the monks' archives show, this was a district known as 'Morgan' which the Anglo-Normans mis-pronounced as 'Margan' and subsequently 'Margam'. It was not however confined to the present village and parish of that name. It incorporated Llangynwyd and the land of the Llynfi Valley, extending south to Newton. Merrick noted that it was described in The Register of Neath as being situated "within the forest of Margam". Bounded by the Avan (Afan) River on the West it most likely extended to the Ogmore River in the east though, as we have seen, the Anglo-Normans had already established a settlement here at Newcastle.

The date of the death of Caradoc ab Iestyn is not known, but is placed (rather dubiously) at 'about 1140'. Both Leslie Evans and Prof Smith therefore concluded that Owain's murder probably had something to do with Earl Robert's annexation of the rest of Margam outside Anglo-Norman control, and my only contribution is to add that this was probably because Owain was in rebellion.

Many years ago (and long before I took a specific interest in the history of the Kenfig district!) I was studying to sit an 'A' Level examination in Medieval History as an adult. Whilst 'mugging up' on the history of the civil war between Stephen and Matilda I came across a reference in one book to the fact that at some stage Stephen's supporters set aside money with a view to bribing Welsh leaders in lands held by those backing the Empress. The idea was to persuade them to rebel thereby opening a 'second front' for her supporters against the Marcher Lords (Earl Robert included). Alas, I never realised its significance at the time, and cannot now recollect the source in question. Such a move made sound sense, though the same source added that there was no evidence the stratagem ever succeeded.

Nevertheless, the circumstances of Owain's death suggest that he may indeed have been preparing to foment an uprising in Glamorgan if he had not done so already. This would explain why Cadwallon was never punished for his brother's murder – unless we accept the monks' view that his subsequent death in battle was the result of divine retribution. He had, presumably, been acting on behalf of Earl Robert to nip the rebellion in the bud. As a rebel Owain's property would have been forfeited to the Earl, his overlord, and this thereby gave Robert the necessary pretext to seize the land of Margam as his own.

Giraldus dates Owain's murder to the year in which he himself had been born, but unfortunately we do not know exactly when that was. It is generally believed to be about 1145-6, a date that fits well with what we know about the Norman arrival at Kenfig and Margam. They were clearly in possession of the district when Earl Robert died in October 1147, but the evidence we have seems to indicate that they had only arrived there fairly recently. Indeed, much of the settlement of Owain's former land appears to have been carried out by Robert's son William, though certainly the idea of establishing a castle and chartered town at Kenfig (duplicating his previous provision for Neath) was Robert's alone.

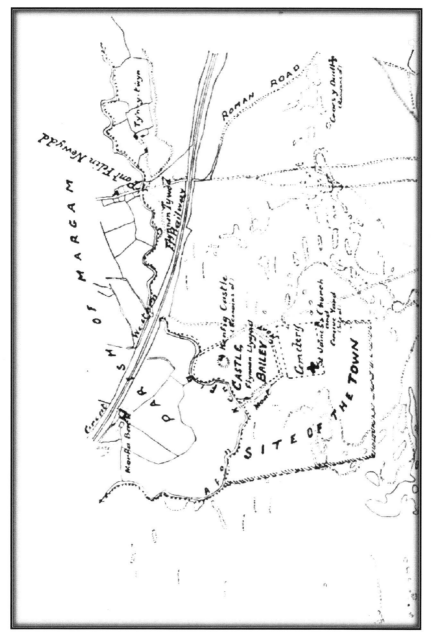

*Map 2: Plan of the site of Kenfig Town, Castle and Church (from Gray, 1909)*

# Chapter 2

## THE TOWN IN THE CASTLE

By the time he died in 1147 we know for certain that Earl Robert had put in place two important elements in the planned Norman occupation of Margam and taken the necessary steps to implement a third. The first two were the construction of the castle and the foundation of a town at Kenfig and at this period of our history the location of the one undoubtedly determined the site of the other. It cannot be stressed too strongly that in the mid 12th century (and for a long time afterwards) the land in which Kenfig stood was wild and untamed country. The settlers found themselves in the midst of a hostile population who spoke a different language and probably made no secret of their intention of driving them out lock, stock and barrel should the opportunity arise.

To the west, at Aberafan, there was Morgan ap Caradoc, the dead Owain's brother, a Welsh chieftain whose intentions the newcomers mistrusted. Although it was true he had not supported Owain's abortive rebellion, but one suspects that he made no secret of his unease about now being hemmed in by the castle at Neath on the one hand and a new one at Kenfig on the other. He may also have been somewhat peeved by the manner in which the Earl had appropriated all of Owain's land for himself without any reward for the rest of the family who may not, like Cadwallon, have actively supported the Earl but had at least not joined their brother's rebellion. Certainly subsequent history was to show that Morgan had designs upon the land of Margam and enjoyed considerable support amongst the Welsh who populated the uplands and valleys around Llangynwyd.

The third element of Earl Robert's settlement – the founding of Margam Abbey in the last weeks of his life – may have been the typical response of a Norman magnate of the era seeking to render his soul more acceptable to God. At the same time it could also be (as Professor Beverly Smith (1958) suggests) an attempt to clothe the iron fist of Kenfig in a velvet glove. The monks were given all the land between the rivers Kenfig and Avan thereby forming a 'demilitarised zone' between Morgan's lordship and the new settlement. Of course the monks could do nothing to prevent one side or the other marching their armies across their property, but it did prevent the kind of day-to-day incidents along a common boundary that could so easily erupt into armed conflict.

As to why the Normans sited their town and castle at Kenfig where they did I am rather puzzled. Given that trouble with both Morgan and the Welsh of the interior was apparently anticipated I would have thought the best location would have been on Mont Mawr – the ridge leading north-east from Mawdlam church. The slope of the ground would have given added strength to their fortifications and commanding views across the countryside to the west and north. There is some evidence indeed that the motte of an abandoned castle existed on this ridge in the early 13th century (see Appendix I). Whether the water supply there was considered inadequate or whether for some other reason, the castle and town were nevertheless sited on low ground right alongside the river Kenfig. Some of my fellow Kenfig Society members have come up with various suggestions for the town's location, one being that the Normans were influenced by the course of the former Roman road[11] which is believed to have crossed the river somewhere in this vicinity. It was whilst searching for evidence to support this that a local man, Graham John stumbled across the site where our

---

[11] I have doubts about this theory which envisages the Romans building their road directly from Mawdlam to Port Talbot across land that was mainly marshes and bog. This would have involved building bridges and embankments that would have been unnecessary if the highway were built further inland along the line of modern Water Street.

archaeological dig was taking place. Another strongly held theory is that it was placed there because the town had a port on the Kenfig estuary. This idea was one that I myself was initially happy to accept but, as time has gone on (and with just about every writer on Kenfig expressing a view to the contrary!), I have come to believe that no such harbour ever in fact existed (see Appendix II).

One practical reason that does commend itself is that by choosing this location the waters of the Kenfig river[12] could be utilised to strengthen the defences of the castle, though I cannot believe that it was built here solely for that reason. Nevertheless, it was a location on the south bank of the river the Normans chose and undoubtedly the castle was the first thing to be built.

This first fortress followed the basic form of a typical 'ringwork' castle of the period[13], the fortifications being at ground level without an artificial mound or 'motte' supporting the keep. This keep was at the heart of the defences and situated inside the inner ward - an oval enclosure created by digging a moat so constructed that the river was diverted around all or some part of it. In the SW corner a gatehouse and drawbridge gave access to the outer enclosure. Although the keep seems to have been built of stone, the gatehouse and remaining fortifications, including those of the outer enclosure, were probably timber. The moat surrounding

---

[12] The river however did not, as has been suggested, exit to the sea via Kenfig Pool (Appendix III)

[13] This description largely follows the excellent one in the RCAHMW 1991 publication *Glamorgan – Early Castles*, Vol III Part 1a, pp 314-326. It in turn is based upon the meagre reports of the excavations carried out by A J Richard (1925). Whilst in most respects this is an excellent description of the castle, its history and background, the RCAHMW report does contain several glaring inaccuracies. Amongst these is the claim that 29 burgages were built at Cefn Cribwr following the abandonment of the town which is an obvious reference to the enclosure of Waun Cimla common in 1572 creating 29 parcels of 'hay' ground. It also repeats the flawed argument that when the castle was built the river Kenfig flowed south to the sea via Kenfig Pool (See Appendix III). Other statements made (such as the one that the enclosed area adjoining the castle was actually the town) are perhaps more a matter of interpretation of the available evidence.

the inner ward was impressive, being some 18m wide (approx 59 feet).

A fragment of a stone capital recovered during excavations within the keep in the 1920s suggests that from the first this tower was built of masonry. At 14m² (about 45½ feet²) it is the largest such castle keep in Glamorgan. The walls were 3.7m thick (12 feet) and it has been estimated that when complete it would have stood to a height of about 18m (59 feet). Mr Richard, the excavator, was of the opinion that the entrance originally stood on the first floor in the west face.

Beyond the inner ward was a large enclosure which the RCAHMW report defines as the enclosure wall of the town. At the same time they admit that, this being the case, its church dedicated to Saint James would have stood outside the defences. Such an arrangement seems highly unlikely to say the least. Much of the boundary bank marking the defences of this enclosure can still be seen. Although partly covered by dunes it is estimated that it encompasses an area of 8¼ acres (3.34ha). Personally I have little doubt that it was indeed the outer ward of the castle[14], but initially it was also almost certainly the location of the town.

This idea was mooted by Professor Ian Soulsby[15] in his 1983 book *The Towns of Medieval Wales* in which he points out that many of the earliest Norman boroughs in Wales often started life within the defences of a castle (Soulsby, 1983: 31-2). Such an arrangement made good sense especially where (as was the case with Kenfig) the new town was planted in newly acquired land with a hostile native population close at hand. The Professor suggests that this may have

---

[14] There is however just a possibility that this enclosure is indeed the town wall and the castle bailey lies somewhere within it, the interior never having been excavated.

[15] Unfortunately Prof Soulsby uses material alleging a pre-Norman origin for Kenfig taken from Thomas Gray's 1909 *Buried City of Kenfig* which actually originates in a chronicle known as the *Gwenllian Brut* now known to be a forgery. No reliable documentary evidence for Kenfig's existence prior to the 1140s in fact exists

been the case at Kenfig, but was not apparently aware that there is actually a strong body of evidence to support his idea.

We know, for example, from later documents that some houses continued in being within the castle defences even after the town was moved outside the castle walls. One was a dwelling that Thomas the son of William of St Donats sold to Robert son of Robert Cauan in the early 13th century (Birch, 1897: 192). This is stated to be within the castle bailey "on the east, near the walls of the cemetery of Kenefeg".

Given the limited space within the inner ward around the keep it is hard to believe that there would have been room for a private house there or even that such would have been tolerated at the heart of the castle's defences. The statement that the wall of the castle adjoined the graveyard within which the church presumably stood also tends to indicate that Robert's new house was within the outer ward.

As the RCAHMW account admits, all available evidence points to the church having stood a long way south of the keep and inner ward. The construction of this church of Saint James also tends to confirm that initially the town was within the castle defences, for it was founded not by Earl Robert, but by his son and successor William. Yet the earliest document that mentions Kenfig town was issued in Robert's day and therefore prior to his death in October 1147. This deed records the grant by Robert to the monks of Ewenny Priory of 21 acres of arable land on Kenfig River, and a burgage lying outside the west gate of the town towards the stream called the Blaklaak (Clark, 1910: CI). It is undated, but the period to which it belongs is determined by the foundation of the Priory in 1141 and Robert's death six years later.

With the town inside the outer ward, this burgage would have lain somewhere in the vicinity of the present excavations by the Kenfig Society, though so far as I have been able to discover, there is no subsequent reference either to it or the arable land. The gate (with its implied defences) would have been part of the castle, and its former location is believed to be indicated by the obvious dip visible in the bank of the outer ward today.

A medieval town without a church would have been unthinkable, but whilst situated within the defences the burgesses would have been able to share the facilities offered by the garrison chapel. This may well be the Chapel of Saint Thomas mentioned at Kenfig in later records but with no clue to identify its location.

Once the community had become sufficiently established to build and man its own defences, it was then moved out of the castle by Earl William who secured the licence for his clerk Henry Thusard to build a church dedicated to Saint James (Clark, 1910: CX) to provide for its spiritual needs. This in turn became the centre of the parish of Kenfig which enables us to say that the transfer took place prior to 1154. A record of that date shows that this was the year when a dispute between Thusard as parson of Saint James and the parish of Kenfig with Job, priest of the parish of Newcastle concerning tithes due from Geoffrey Sturmy was formally concluded by the Archbishop of Canterbury (PM 378).

What seems to finally clinch the argument regarding the location of the early town within the castle defences and its subsequent removal is a series of apparently conflicting statements made by our old friend Rice Merrick from his research with the lost register of Neath Abbey. In one place in his history he states that Earl Robert founded the town of Kenfig (Merrick, 1578: 42, 101) then elsewhere credits this to his son William (Merrick, 1578: 20). Yet a third entry when taken in conjunction with Soulsby's suggestion does nevertheless enable us to reconcile these two apparently conflicting statements (Merrick, 1578: 42).

> This William (son of Earl Robert) caused to be rebuilded a town for merchandise upon the seabanks of Kenfig, which he retained, with [a] certain parcel of land thereto belonging, in his own possession.

This seems to confirm that the town of Kenfig that was founded by Robert existed within the outer bailey of Kenfig castle prior to 1147 and was then 'rebuilded' outside the walls by his successor by the year 1154. Reference to a 'burgage' in Earl Robert's charter to Ewenny Priory also indicates that despite its lowly origins this early town was indeed from the first a chartered borough, and its leading citizens were burgesses ruled over by a Portreeve in the manner of their successors.

One final element of this first town also seems to be mentioned in later charters, and this is the graveyard. The inhabitants may have been able to use the garrison chapel as their place of worship, but it can well be imagined that the Constable of the Castle would not have been keen to have burials within his fortress. What was probably the community's original burial ground outside the castle walls is alluded to in a grant (PM 105)[16] of ten acres of land to Margam Abbey by Gilbert Grammus who died circa 1202/3. These ten acres[17] lay in a bend of the river Kenfig which bounded it on three sides with an 'old cemetery' on the south forming the fourth[18]. The location of this land was apparently known as late as 1633 when the property is described in virtually identical terms in a survey of the manor of Higher Kenfig (PM 1280). The jurors mentioned that they had taken the details from an older survey of 1582 and were at pains to point out that although the land lay on the south side of the river Kenfig it had always been considered part and parcel of the Margam manor of Higher Kenfig.

I would suspect that this burial ground lay to the west of the entrance to the outer ward of the castle which would have provided

---

[16] Thomas Gray (1909) believed this land lay on the eastern side of the town, but his reasoning for placing it there is flawed.

[17] The medieval acre in use in the district was about two-thirds the size of the modern equivalent, so the actual area of the field was probably slightly less than 7 acres modern measure.

[18] The use of the term 'old cemetery' makes it clear that this was not the graveyard of St James' church as this was in use at the time the deed was written. ['Higher Kenfig' consists of lands alongside today's Water Street, and will be explained later in Chapter 9. (ed.)]

convenient access to it from the early town. In fact I think it may well have been the land we now call 'Castle Meadow' even though today this lies on the north side of a ribbon lake marking an old abandoned meander of the river. The Kenfig river has changed course so many times over the past centuries that back in 1633 its course may well have lain further north.

The event that persuaded Earl William that the time had come to move the town out of the castle defences was perhaps a Welsh invasion that occurred in 1153.

**Site of Kenfig old town today.**
*Note Swansea Bay and the Port Talbot steel works
in the background*

Rhys ap Tewdwr, who had ruled or controlled most of South Wales, was killed at the battle of Brecon in 1093, and the Normans then overran much of his land including Glamorgan. A Welsh counter-offensive subsequently regained control of most of the upland territory but was unable to dislodge the invaders from the lowland areas. Gryffydd, son of the dead prince, therefore managed to survive as ruler of certain lands in the upper part of the Cothi valley in Carmarthenshire. From time to time he launched raids upon the Norman settlers such as one in 1136 when he combined with Owain Gwynedd, Prince of North Wales to win a battle against the Normans at Crug Mawr near Cardigan.

With England preoccupied with the civil war between Stephen and Matilda, his sons, Cadell, Maredudd and Rhys were able to build upon their father's modest success. In 1146 they captured the castles at Carmarthen and Llanstephan, then in 1150 raided the area around Kidwelly and the Gower. The burgesses of Kenfig would have turned anxious eyes westwards at this news, especially as Gwladys, the mother of Morgan ap Caradoc of Avan, was a sister to the brothers. In the event the three turned their attention instead to Ceredigion (Cardigan) which had originally been part of their grandfather's principality of Deheubarth but had since been appropriated by Hywel the son of Owain Gwynedd. It took them two years to drive him out and during the campaign Cadell was so seriously injured that he was unable to play any part in subsequent events.

In 1153, and with Ceredigion safely in their hands, Maredudd and Rhys turned their attention once more to the Anglo-Norman settlements of the south and east. Having captured Tenby and burnt St Clears, they then led their forces towards Glamorgan. As news filtered through, it became increasingly obvious to the Kenfig burgesses that this time their town would be directly in the path of the brothers and their army. If their town was still in the outer ward at this time its defences were actually fairly substantial. A portion of the ditch excavated by Richard (RCAHMW, 1991: 325) shows that it was 14.7m wide and 4.3m deep (48½ ft x 14ft) and behind it was a bank of boulder clay and river pebbles surmounted by a wooden palisade. The problem, of course, was of the sheer size of the perimeter to be defended!

Maredudd and Rhys apparently by-passed the fortress and town of Neath, but then halted at Aberafan, the stronghold of their nephew Morgan. The burgesses waited with growing trepidation, but the news, when it came, was probably as unexpected for them as it is inexplicable to us today. The two brothers attacked Aberafan castle, killed the garrison, set it on fire, then calmly turned round and headed back from whence they came!

This is such an amazing occurrence that the author of the RCAHMW (1991: 155) report on the long vanished castle at Aberafan suggests that perhaps the fortress was in Norman hands at the time! What it suggests to me, however, is that at this stage in his life Morgan ap Caradoc was not prepared to co-operate with his uncles in their campaign against the Normans. Either the attack was deliberately targeted at Aberafan to 'persuade' him to change his mind, or Maredudd and Rhys had been counting on his support for a planned attack on Kenfig and the settlements in the Vale of Glamorgan, and had been rebuffed. Either way Earl William can have been left in no doubt that they were displaying a keen interest in the affairs of his territory, and it was perhaps at this stage that Kenfig town was moved out of the castle bailey.

I have a theory (but one based on very little evidence) that the Earl may have intended to use the area of the outer ward as a muster point and depot for operations against the growing power of the sons of Gryffydd or possibly even Morgan ap Caradoc. Earl William would have had a few professional soldiers at his command but the vast majority of any army he could raise would have been made up of his tenants. These professionals were the knights of the Shire Fee who were generally mounted and well armed, but accompanying each would be a number of 'rank and file' soldiers drawn from their own tenants and peasantry. Not to put too fine a point on it these were usually poorly equipped and on the field of battle were, what a later age would bluntly refer to as 'cannon fodder'.

When summoned, each knight with his band of followers made their way to a pre-arranged muster point and once all were gathered the army would move off to the scene of the action. For the

Anglo-Normans of Glamorgan this tended to be either east towards England, or west along the coast in the direction of Gower. Cardiff Castle with the adjacent town provided an ideal depot for such a collection point in the east – the knights of the shire even had their own houses within the eastern ward for accommodation when required to perform castle-guard or attend courts in the adjoining shire hall. But what if the muster was made for operations in the west? A gathering at Cardiff made little sense for De Londres of Ogmore or the Turbervilles of Coity when they were required to gather for operations in West Wales.

The Earl's fortress at Newcastle was too small to serve this purpose and in any case could be rendered temporarily inaccessible if the river Ogmore was in spate and the ford impassable. Initially (and subsequently) I believe Ewenny Priory may have fulfilled this purpose, and that this is the reason for it being fortified. In 1153 the Earl may however have decided that the role could be fulfilled by Kenfig castle. With the townsfolk removed from the outer ward there was now a large fortified enclosure in which the Glamorgan feudal levy could muster and in which supplies for the operation could be stored.

Unfortunately, as we shall see, Kenfig itself became the focus for much of the military action that took place during the years that followed, and was consequently often in the heart of hostile territory. Small bands of soldiers making their way through this would have simply been picked off one by one. By the end of the century a return had been made to Ewenny, sheltered by the fortresses of the Lower Ogmore. Significantly perhaps the earliest stone fortifications there do indeed date from that period.

The burgesses, incidentally, were excused service in the Earl's feudal array. He had them right where he wanted them – a Norman bastion in what was to become the 'front line' for the next century and more. The affair at Aberafan meant that Kenfig's first major crisis had fizzled out into an anti-climax. Nevertheless events were already in train that would soon prove the burgesses' freedom from military service was no empty sinecure.

So much therefore for the town of Kenfig itself, but it would be wrong of me to continue this history by viewing it in isolation without reference to the area in which it was situated. Kenfig was, as Merrick says, "a town for merchandise", and its burgesses were a collection of craftspeople, shopkeepers and merchants whose livelihood depended on their relationship with those in the surrounding district. It was from here they drew their raw materials, and to its inhabitants that they sold their wares. The need to secure a living through trade in these unpromising surroundings meant dealing not only with those of their own race who now settled the surrounding land but, however reluctantly, with their Welsh neighbours as well.

# Chapter 3

## THE LAND CALLED MORGAN

The town and borough of Kenfig, the castle and the Abbey of Margam were just elements in a comprehensive plan for the occupation of the land of Morgan initiated by Earl Robert and carried through under his son William. The full title of the Anglo-Norman lords that subsequently held sway at Cardiff castle was 'Lords of Glamorgan and Morgan', and that last element seems to reflect that Owain's former lordship was not immediately incorporated into their other property but treated as a separate entity. This seems to be confirmed by an early charter in the Margam collection that speaks of "all the Welsh Hundred of the County of Margan" (Birch, 1897: 26).

This phase appears to have passed quite quickly, and was followed by one where the land between the Avan (Afan) and Ogmore rivers was treated as a member lordship, or at least a separate territory within Glamorgan over which Earl William claimed lordship. It is then generally referred to as 'the land of Margam' or 'The Earl's fee in Margam'.

The upheavals that occurred here following the Earl's death in 1183 saw another change in status whereby the concept of Margam as a single entity was abolished and the various constituents within it became separate units within the lordship of Glamorgan. Earl Gilbert de Clare who took control circa 1218 apparently brought this about as part of a general reorganisation of the lordship, something that will be dealt with more fully in due course. Suffice is to say here that the former Land of Margam subsequently continued to exist only as an administrative unit known as The Hundred of Kenfig. This remained in being even after the abandonment of Kenfig in the 15th century, but was reorganised as The Hundred of Newcastle in the time of Henry VIII.

As it existed in the 12th century the Land of Margam consisted of four main elements – the lowland settlements; the predominately Welsh uplands; Kenfig Territory; and the land of Margam Abbey.

The distribution of the lowland settlements was largely influenced by the fact that much of the underlying rock in the district is porous limestone. Along the coast, between Laleston and the lower reaches of the Kenfig river the sole stream is the fitful Candleston Brook which manages to flow only after prolonged periods of rain. When the first Anglo-Normans moved into the district the availability of a reliable water supply therefore dictated where they built their villages and settlements. Some, like Newcastle, Merthyr Mawr, Llangewydd, and Kenfig adjoined rivers and streams, whilst others were situated at locations on the perimeter of the limestone cap of Newton/Stormy Down. There are no streams or standing water on the Down itself. Rainwater percolates through cracks and fissures in the rock until it reaches a band of clay that underlies it. Unable to penetrate further, it emerges at the base of the Down in the form of springs, seeps and shallow wells, and it is at these locations that many of our earliest villages are situated.

## The Lowland Settlements

**Newcastle (**in Bridgend). As has already been mentioned this was undoubtedly the first Anglo-Norman settlement within Margam, and was in being by 1106. It takes its name from the fact that there was an older castle (Oldcastle) on the opposite side of the river in the Turberville lordship of Coity.

The purpose of these castles initially was to protect the ford crossing the river Ogmore at this point, and probably oversee traffic.

on the main Cardiff road into and from the Welsh territory further west. As late as the end of the 12th century the main highway ran from Ewenny Bridge to Oldcastle then, having crossed the river, ascended Newcastle Hill to the castle. Beneath its walls it then turned west to Laleston along what was Llangewydd Lane the course of which has been much altered by modern housing developments.

***'New'-Castle and Church in Bridgend***
*on a bluff overlooking the town and river Ogmore*

The settlement at Newcastle was probably the largest after Kenfig in the Land of Margam, and possibly like Kenfig it was initially situated within the outworks of the castle. This idea occurred to me when considering the proximity of the church to the castle, and the way in which both it and its surrounding graveyard seems to occupy a ledge cut into the slope. Perhaps originally this was the site of a village that was later moved leaving the church in sole possession.

**Merthyr Mawr.** There was some sort of ecclesiastical establishment here long before the Normans arrived in Glamorgan, but its early history is obscure. The occurrence of the names 'Quentin's Wood' and 'Quentin's Barn' have suggested to some that it was originally a manor belonging to the De St Quentin family of Llanblethian whose successors certainly held it in the mid 13th century. It contained within it a sub-manor based upon a settlement at **Candleston** which was subsequently abandoned in the face of sand encroachment leaving just a ruined 14th century fortified mansion as mute witness to its former existence.

*Tythegeston Church*

**Tythegston.** Later in the medieval period there is ample evidence that this was a sub-manor of Newcastle based upon a manor house that may have been fortified and probably stood on the present site of Tythegston Court. The church of Saint Tyddwg certainly pre-dates the conquest, but whether a settlement existed here in the late 12th century is debatable

**Newton** (now in Porthcawl). The first settlement here was established by Richard de Cardiff on land given to him by Earl William of Gloucester post-1166[19]. Newton is unique amongst Glamorgan manors in that a copy of its foundation charter has survived, though it is a very curious document (Birch, 1897: 39) which poses as many questions as it answers. It was copied from the original by a Margam scribe following a dispute between De Cardiff and the Abbot over whether the latter owed him service for land the Abbey had acquired in the vicinity of Sker. This was resolved by reference to the Earl who confirmed that he had given the monks their land before his charter to Richard, and therefore the latter had no jurisdiction over it.

The main difficulty with this charter is that it describes a manor of far greater extent than Newton subsequently encompassed. Not only did it include the territory of the parish of Newton Nottage[20], but that of Pyle & Kenfig as well. Kenfig and its

---

[19] The occurrence of this document in the Margam archive is undoubtedly tied to the dispute between the Abbey and Richard de Cardiff, and it is on this basis that this date is suggested. The 100 acres at Sker was given to the monks in exchange for a burgage at Newborough (the location of which is uncertain) formerly belonging to Baldwin the Harper (PM 25). Neither of these properties are mentioned in King Henry's confirmation charter to the Abbey circa 1156, so are therefore presumably subsequent to it. Bishop Nicholas of Llandaff (HC A 15) states that the Abbot won his case by showing that his Abbey had possessed the property for upwards of ten years before Richard de Cardiff's grant, so we are looking at a date post 1166. It is unlikely to have been very much later.

[20] One of the main problems that subsequent writers have had interpreting this document is that Birch in his 1897 book *Margam Abbey* (p.39) suggested that the 'Dewiscumbe' mentioned in the charter was the valley adjoining St David's Well at Nottage. On the name alone this appears perfectly logical, but the subsequent recitation of the boundary is

sub-manors at North and South Cornelly would have therefore been within its borders, though all three were probably already in existence when the Newton charter was sealed. As Earl William's ruling in the case of Margam's land at Sker illustrates, these too would presumably have been outside Richard's control. Following the events of 1167-85 the subsequent lords of Newton probably lost their northern territory and were afterwards unable or disinclined to secure its return.

**Nottage.** Although generally considered to be an older community than neighbouring Newton, no firm evidence has so far emerged to show that a settlement was in existence here in the 12th century.

**Sker.** This was a monastic grange (or farm) centred upon what is now Sker House. The original gift of land to Neath Abbey at 'Blakeskarra' was made by Robert Earl of Gloucester (Merrick, 1578: 42)[21] and subsequently supplemented by the purchase of the land from Margam Abbey that provoked the dispute with Richard de Cardiff.

**South Cornelly.** Thomas Gray in his 1909 *Buried City of Kenfig* claimed, in a typical burst of enthusiasm, that the village got its name from the dedication of the chapel there to a Breton saint named Cornelius. Let it be said here and now that **this claim has no basis in fact.** Whilst I gladly pay tribute to Thomas Gray for his pioneering work on Kenfig and district, unfortunately he often allowed his imagination free rein with disastrous results! This is just

---

impossible to relate to the landscape. If, on the other hand, Dewiscumbe is identified with 'Happy Valley' on the eastern edge of the parish of Newton Nottage, then the subsequent sequence of boundary marks makes better sense and follows the parish boundary northwards to its border with Pyle & Kenfig.

[21] Merrick seems to have obtained this information from a charter granting Neath Abbey land at 'Blacksker' by William Earl of Gloucester. This is unlikely to be the hundred acres acquired from Margam as that was simply a business transaction between the two houses.

one example, but like several others it has become so deeply ingrained into the popular psyche that it is still with us today.

What old Thomas read was an extract from an undated list of Glamorgan churches and chapels confirmed to Tewkesbury Abbey by Bishop Nicholas of Llandaff who died in 1183 (Gray, 1909: 70). This includes "The chapel of Corneli which is Thom's Town". To Gray it seemed that the writer had omitted to prefix the name Cornelly with 'St', so having discovered a possible candidate, he rectified the 'error'! It is in fact more likely that the name stems from the Welsh 'cornel' meaning a corner or angle and refers to the bends made by the dry valley at the location where the village stands. The earliest lords of the manor were a family that eventually took the name 'de Cornelly' of whom the Thomas (after whom the settlement was so nearly named) was one of the earliest on record.

**North Cornelly.** How and why the name Cornelly attached itself to this settlement is unknown, though the process was well advanced by the middle of the 13th century. The Bishop Nicholas list of churches and chapels calls it 'Lupelluston' after the family name of the lords of the manor here. Their surname means 'wolf' which is the badge that appears on a seal attached to a document in the Margam collections, though by this time they had changed it to 'Lovel'. Their chapel here was dedicated to Saint Wenduin who was, so far as anyone can discover, an obscure Germanic saint who was the patron of sheep. Who says our medieval forebears didn't have a sense of humour?! Like its neighbour to the south, North Cornelly was a sub-manor held from Kenfig.

**Stormy.** A manor and village was founded here prior to 1154 by Geoffrey Sturmy, a younger son of the Esturmy family of Wiltshire who were the hereditary wardens of the royal forest of Savernake[22].

---

[22] For fuller details of this family and their settlement see my unpublished 1990 book *Sturmi's Land*, copies of which have been deposited with Bridgend Library.

They are known to have built a chapel and a village called 'Sturmiestown' which I believe was situated alongside a track marking the northern edge of the common today. The position is complicated however by the fact that a second village grew up here in the 16th century, so only by excavation would it be possible to determine that some of the hut sites apparent today are actually of medieval origin.

Perhaps it was because of the distance from both Newcastle and Kenfig that the family also built a small castle to give shelter to themselves and their villagers. Its remains have been subject to much vandalism over the years – part of the motte or mound that supported the keep having evidently been used to fill up the encircling ditch. Originally therefore it was a rather more imposing structure than the present rather sorry surviving remnant might suggest.

This castle stands on a spur of land on the northern side of Stormy Down from which it is separated by a shallow valley. So far as can be ascertained it was simply an artificial mound encompassed by a ditch upon which would have stood a wooden tower or keep with an entrance on the first floor reached via a ladder. There are no indications of any outer defences.

Although presumably (and primarily) for the protection of Geoffrey Sturmy and his people his castle was also strategically situated so as to keep an eye upon an ancient trackway that connected Stormy Down to Cefn Cribwr along a narrow watershed ridge that divides the valley at this point

**Llangewydd.** The manor of the Scurlage family: this settlement lay north of Laleston, and the former village here is believed to lie a little to the east of the hump-backed railway-bridge on the Laleston to Cefn Cribwr road. One of the earliest grants made to Margam Abbey was of land at Llangewydd by a certain Roger de Albertona or Haubertunia (there are various renderings of the name) shortly after 1147. Whether he was the original lord of the manor or just a tenant of the Scurlages is unclear, but certainly the latter were on the scene very shortly afterwards.

The eminent historian Prof F.G. Cowley claims (Cowley, 1977: 80-1) on the basis of a story told by Giraldus Cambrensis about an unnamed manor in Wales that the Scurlages also had a castle here, though no trace of one remains today. My own feeling however is that the tale is more likely to relate to neighbouring Stormy.

**Laleston.** The last of these early settlements in the Land of Margam was the home of, and takes its name from, the Lageles family. Walter Lageles was given land here by Earl William (Birch, 1897:53) and his descendant Thomas donated some of it to Margam Abbey sometime between 1186 and 1204. It is this latter document that contains the particularly interesting information that the road through the village was then part of the main highway connecting Cardiff to Kenfig (Birch, 1897: 152).

**Isolated Homesteads.** As well as the villages there were scattered throughout the district isolated farmsteads that were home to just a single family. Of these three can be identified from the Margam archives. **Grove** (originally Burdin's Grove) is the former farm of that name on the road between South Cornelly and Nottage and was the home of the Burdin family who were contemporaries of the Sturmies and connected to them by marriage.

Gilbert Grammus, whose descendants later inhabited **Marlas Farm**, Pyle, is mentioned in 1183/4 and was presumably living there then. **Catteputte** (modern Pwllygath, Kenfig Hill) is mentioned in the charter creating the manor of Newton. Gistelard, the descendant of a man named John or Joaf granted land here to Margam no later than 1206, but establishing the identity of the earliest landholders has so far proved rather difficult.

**The Uplands.**

As I tracked the history of settlements in the upland areas of Margam a strange story emerged regarding the distribution of land here in the initial stages of the Anglo-Norman settlement. It is clear that whilst Earl Robert and his son William were content to allow the native population to live according to their own laws and customs, one or two Anglo-Norman families were nevertheless introduced into the district. Two in particular – Herbert son of Godwinett and Gillemichel (probably a Welsh form of 'Gilbert son of Michael') – are particularly prominent. The story of Herbert and his sons also reveals the monks of Margam in none too an agreeable light.

When Earl Robert of Gloucester gave the Cistercian Order permission to found an abbey at Margam he also endowed the new community with a generous amount of land. As described in the charter (of Hugh le Despenser in which the text of the original is preserved), it extended from Kenfig River to the river Avan, and inland from the coast to "the brow of the mountains" (Birch, 1897: .13). It is this latter phrase that was to subsequently cause problems. However much can be said in favour of the Cistercian monks, they had one serious deficiency in that they were very acquisitive, and Giraldus Cambrensis, who was otherwise greatly impressed by the good work being done by the community at Margam, later castigated the Order for this aspect of its character.

Having settled themselves in at their new home, it was not long before the monks began exploring their new territory and, since the rules of their Order forbade them to have lay tenants, they moved out any whose homes or land lay within their borders. It was not too long before differences arose between the Abbot and Earl William of Gloucester over the interpretation of that phrase "the brow of the mountains". The latter took it to refer to the brow of the hills immediately behind the monastery, but the monks were quick to point out that when one stood at the top of these hills there was higher ground further inland that still lay between the two rivers.

At stake was the future of those families who held land within the borders of this disputed territory. Events had already shown that if the Abbot won his case they would be kicked off their land without further ado. Amongst them were Herbert and his family who had a holding at Gallt-y-Cwm ('Killeculum') high up in the Cwm Dyffryn (Ffrwdwyllt) valley. He had apparently settled here quite happily and married a local girl of Welsh origin for their sons bear a mixture of English and Welsh names. When Herbert died the Earl issued a charter (Birch, 1897: 49) to four of these (there were at least seven in all) confirming their possession of Gallt-y-Cwm, and armed with this document they may well have believed that their tenancy was perfectly secure. But then William caved in to the Abbot's demands.

In a face-saving move he gave the disputed land to his young son Robert who in turn gave it to the monks (Birch, 1897: 40-1). The date this took place is determined by the fact that Robert died in 1166 at the age of sixteen, and perhaps the destruction of an Abbey barn by arson in 1161 was actually a protest against the Abbey's claims by the hapless population.

The Herberts cannot have been the only family affected. Their story is, however, apparent in the Abbey records because they continued the fight to recover Gallt-y-Cwm for several generations before finally admitting defeat and surrendering Earl William's charter to the monks. Interestingly these later generations are often difficult to identify because despite their ancestry they all bore Welsh names, and identified themselves with the native population. In the circumstances this might have come about as a reaction to their treatment by the Earl, but the same cannot be said of the descendants of Gillemichel.

Their principal holding lay at Gelli Lenor north of Llangynwyd (near Maesteg) in the land of Tir Iarll, though it is documents relating to some property they acquired in the vicinity of Kenfig Hill and Cefn Cribwr that enables us to trace their subsequent history. Like Herbert in neighbouring Gallt-y-Cwm,

Gillimichel seems to have married into a Welsh family and his two sons were named William and Cadrawd. Again like the Herberts the Gillemichel descendants gave their children Welsh names and became so closely identified with the native population that Gilbert de Clare turned them out of their property on Cefn Cribwr when he ejected other 'free Welshmen of Kenfig' post 1218.

Elsewhere, Welshmen in the hills who had not been overtly hostile to the Normans were allowed to retain their land and undoubtedly formed the bulk of the population. Earl William seems to have been content to allow them to keep their own laws and customs, though to ensure their good behaviour he probably built the first castle at Llangynwyd. Some of the earliest features of the ruins there today seem to date from the second half of the 12th century though its existence in the records cannot be confirmed prior to 1257.

## The Territory of Kenfig

The later feudal Manor of Kenfig originated as a 'Territory' of that name which covered an area slightly larger than the modern parish of Pyle & Kenfig. Within it lay the sub-manors of North and South Cornelly together with Kenfig Borough. Beyond these elements however the land seems to have been but sparsely populated.

Local readers will no doubt have picked up on the fact that I have not included Mawdlam in my review of settlements earlier in this chapter, but the omission is quite deliberate for it is my belief that it did not come into existence until the 15th century. In one respect this flies in the face of existing evidence: it is clear from old maps as well as certain documents that the land here was in cultivation during the medieval period. On the maps the shape of the fields betray their origin as strips of land typical of medieval agriculture.

Also at this location there was a chapel dedicated to Saint Mary Magdalene, which was in being by the middle of the 13th century, and would therefore seem to indicate the existence of a village. Recent research, however, indicates that it was probably in fact part of a leper hospital, and that once this went out of use the chapel fell into ruin. This research is set out in Appendix VI, and tends to indicate that no settlement existed on Heol Las prior to the 15th century. Although Mawdlam therefore lay outside their boundary, the medieval field systems here were probably created by burgesses from the medieval town.

Similarly, prior to the 15th century there is no mention of any settlement at Pyle, nor in fact any indication of a road here along the line of the present A48. A road from Margam Abbey is presumed to have crossed the river Kenfig at Pyle bridge, but apparently led up to Catteputte (Pwllygath in Kenfig Hill), and then on to the Abbey granges at Stormy and Llangewydd. At the other end of the present village a ford called 'Redesice' (Rhyd y Sais – The English Ford) is mentioned in a document belonging to the period 1186-1218 (Birch, 1897: 47). This, however, was apparently only used by the inhabitants of North Cornelly to gain access to land in the 'Culture of Deumay' (Birch, 1897: 188) which adjoined the Afan Fach in the vicinity of modern Beach Road.

It is also significant that in contemporary documents the road from Marlas to Cefn Cribwr is generally referred to as leading from Kenfig to Cefn Cribwr (alias 'The Rugge') or Catteputte without any mention of any intervening settlement in the vicinity of what became Pyle Cross.

**The Borough of Kenfig** lay within this territory or manor of Kenfig, but retained its own laws and customs and was distinct from it. At this early stage in its history it only encompassed a fairly small area lying between Mawdlam Church and the river Kenfig.

A detailed picture of the town, its life and its government is included elsewhere (in Chapter 8), so at this stage I will merely stress that life for those living here was completely different from that of the ordinary people of the surrounding district. Within its borders the population was ruled by a Portreeve, appointed annually and advised by a council of Aldermen. The community made its own laws and, if the Portreeve and Constable of the Castle agreed, could declare laws that were currently in force outside its borders null and void within them. The population held its own courts, and by and large administered its own judicial system. Those who were burgesses were the ruling elite of the community. They were free men, and they enjoyed rights and privileges that were denied to most ordinary folk in the surrounding district.

Just as the town of Kenfig was the social and commercial centre of the Norman settlement of Margam, as was the case throughout England and Wales the townsfolk were regarded with envy not only by the Welsh, but also their own countrymen.

## The Abbey of Margam

The Abbey lands ruled by the Abbot of Margam roughly coincided with the present Parish of Margam and therefore bordered Kenfig Borough along the river. Kenfig River is little more than a large stream, but the contrast between the lay settlements on the one side and the Abbey land on the other was quite stark.

At the time the community was established in 1147 the monasteries of the Cistercian Order were not permitted to have lay tenants either renting or working their land. This is the reason why the Herberts and others were ejected from the disputed land north of the monastery once Earl William of Gloucester had conceded possession. The idea was that the monks should not become lazy and idle, but instead would work the land they owned with their own hands and by the sweat of their own brows.

In the event this led to the creation of two types of monks within the Order. One lived the sort of life we normally associate with monastic communities – a daily round of prayers coupled with certain charitable duties and creating illuminated manuscripts in the abbey scriptorium. Alongside them worked the 'conversii' or lay-brethren. Whilst also observing the daily prayers, these were often illiterate, and their offering to God was the work of their hands.

Most were employed on the abbey's farms or 'granges' carved out of the land they had been given and considered to be the first true farms to appear in Britain.

One of the largest of these granges (which played an important part in Kenfig's later history) was that of St Michael which today is better known as Llanmihangel. In a return to the parent house at Clairvaux in 1336 (Birch, 1897: 304) the Abbot of Margam says that the land cultivated by this grange amounted to 7 caracutes plus 29 acres of meadow. A caracute was an unit of 120 acres, but since the medieval acre in use locally was smaller than the modern one, its area would actually have been about 580 acres. This nevertheless placed it amongst the top three Margam granges in terms of size. With regard to the value of the land it contained it was second only to the larger one at Llangewydd.

The former grange buildings stood on the slope leading down to the present Llanmihangel Farm from the east, and virtually all trace has now vanished. It would have consisted of living accommodation for the lay-brethren, a chapel at which they could hold their services, and associated farm buildings of which the barn was the last surviving feature. This burnt down in the late 20th century leaving just a few fragments of walls standing forlornly amongst the building complex there.

Associated with the grange were two mills: one of these is believed to have been a fulling-mill for processing woollen cloth. The other was Llanmihangel corn mill which still exists today but in a sadly decayed and dilapidated condition. Other than these and the farm-fields, the land immediately north the river was just unimproved waste, and this continued to be the case even after the Cistercian's relaxed their embargo on lay tenants in 1220. The one exception may have been a house at Ty'n y Cellar. The name of this farm is, in its present form nonsensical – 'The House in the Cellar' – so it is thought that perhaps it originally derives from the fact that it may have belonged to the Abbey's Cellarer. He was an important official who had charge of the community's stores, but such a connection is a possibility and no more.

In its report on medieval granges in Glamorgan the Royal Commission on Ancient & Historical Monuments in Wales (1982: 245-) claims that Eglwys Nunnydd Farm which lay just beyond the border of the later enlarged Borough of Kenfig was another monastic grange called 'Llanvigeilydd' (RCAHMW, 1982: 279-80). Mentions of this grange however only occur in Abbey charters of the early 16th century, and documents relating to a shipwreck on its land (PM 5030-1; 5728; 5800 & 6078) show that it adjoined the coast. Furthermore, later Margam estate documents show that whilst Eglwys Nunnydd lay in the manor of Middle Margam, Llanvigeilydd was in Havod y Porth. Despite the discovery in 1987 of the remains of a 13th century chapel incorporated into the fabric of Eglwys Nunnydd farmhouse, the two are evidently not identical[23].

---

[23] My own research made at the time of the discovery of these remains in fact led me to believe that Llanvigellydd Grange was an amalgamation of the property of Theodoric's grange together with those at Upper Court and Mieles Grange.

# Chapter 4

## CONFLICT IN GLAMORGAN

The Civil War in England effectively came to an end in 1153 when Matilda's son Henry, who had assumed leadership of the rebel faction, met King Stephen at Winchester on the 6th of November. They concluded an agreement whereby Stephen was allowed to reign in peace for the remainder of his life but with Henry as his acknowledged heir. On the 13th of January the chief nobles of the Kingdom met Stephen at Oxford, and by his command did homage to Henry as their lord, saving only the honour and fealty they owed to Stephen as their sovereign. Later that year, in October, Stephen became violently ill and died on the 25th. Henry, who had left the kingdom in April, returned and was duly crowned as Henry II at Westminster on the 19th of December. The great civil war was over.

In South-East Wales there now broke out a conflict which was largely ignored by the chroniclers of the time and by Welsh historians since, despite the fact that it was to continue off and on for some 75 years. The Welsh chroniclers of the day were concerned only with events involving the great princely houses of Gwynedd, Powys and Deheubarth, but this was a local war involving Welsh chieftains still holding out in Glamorgan, Gwent and Breconshire. The events marking its progress only therefore rated a mention by the chroniclers when their patrons were involved and similarly Anglo-Norman annalists were interested only when the Crown took a hand in events.

That this conflict involved only the native chieftains and Marcher Lords makes it of only passing interest to historians interested mainly in 'the big picture'. The abiding impression I get is that because of the fragmentary nature of the available information they generally tended to view outbreaks in the South-East almost as a case of 'the Welsh being Welsh'. Yet, when all the strands are drawn together they tell a coherent story of how the fighting started and why it continued for such a long period. It was not a continuous conflict. Outbreaks flared up and died down; there were truces and temporary peace settlements; but the 'rebellions' that occurred during the 1220s and 1230s were a direct result of events during the twenty year period between 1167 and 1187 which in turn were sparked off by a series of local incidents perpetrated by Earl William of Gloucester as soon as the Civil War came to an end.

After his father Robert's death in 1147, the Glamorgan overlord, Earl William, continued his support for the rebel cause in England though it would be true to say that he was a far more ineffective character. The end of hostilities meant however that he could turn his attention to a task that was apparently close to his heart – eliminating once and for all the semi–independent Welsh lords that still held sway not only in the uplands of Glamorgan but on his estates in Lower Gwent. It is known, for example, that in the 1150s and early 1160s he appropriated large amounts of territory from the Welsh. We know that he seized part of the Welsh Lordship of Senghenydd which stretched from Whitchurch and Rhiwbina on the north of Cardiff right to the Breconshire border.

In Gwent he seized the Welsh hill-lordship of Gwynllwg which shared a boundary with Senghenydd along the Rhymney river. Iorwerth ab Owain was ejected from Caerleon, and (although the evidence is rather scanty) it seems that it was during this period that the De St Quentin family of Llanblethian drove the Welsh out of the lordship of Ruthin which lay about St Mary Hill and Llanharry. It can be demonstrated that at the time of Earl Robert's death it was in the hands of a certain Rhys ab Iestyn, but had probably changed hands by the year 1166.

There is also a possibility that William appropriated a portion of Avan Lordship where Port Talbot and Aberafan now stand, thereby securing the overland link between Kenfig and his isolated outpost at Neath. The evidence for this rests upon a grant by the Earl to William FitzHenry preserved in the charters of Gloucester Abbey of land at Aberafan (RCAHMW, 1991: 155). The document is undated, but interestingly FitzHenry is also connected with an exchange of land at Gelligarn by a certain Simon de Halwaya with Neath Abbey for land in Devon. Merrick (1578: 58), drawing upon his research from the lost Register of Neath Abbey says that this exchange was made because Simon had been "disgraced and spoiled by the Welshmen, his neighbours of Rhuthin, and so brought to extreme poverty". This shows that FitzHenry was current in Glamorgan shortly before Ruthin was appropriated by the De St Quentins and when it was still in Welsh hands.

In the case of the Earl's seizure of part of Senghenydd, its lord, Ivor Bach forced its return by a daring raid on Cardiff Castle in 1157 when he successfully abducted the Earl, his wife and their only son from under the noses of the garrison. Spiriting them off into the mountains he then dictated his own terms for the return of his property before releasing them unharmed.

What was going on in Glamorgan was being repeated in neighbouring Gwent, and it was obviously only a matter of time before the Welsh reacted. The only surprise is that they apparently held back until 1167 when we get the first indication of violence marked by an attack on Kenfig that left the town in ashes.

The Welsh leader is not named, but if Morgan ap Caradoc of Avan did not actually lead the attack at the head of his men, we can be pretty certain from subsequent events that he played a major part in promoting it! In this he was aided by the Welsh of Tir Iarll (to the north of Margam: see Map 1, p.16), including no doubt several families (the sons of Herbert amongst them) who had just lost their land in the mountains north of Margam when the Earl ceded that territory to the monks.

Although details are extremely sketchy the situation in South-East Wales over the next few years became so unstable that it attracted the notice of King Henry II. During the winter of 1171-2 he invaded Ireland to established Norman rule in and around Dublin, and rein in 'Strongbow', the maverick Richard de Clare who had invaded independently from Pembroke Castle in 1169. This in turn gave added weight to his concerns about South Wales: for now the coastal road to Pembroke formed an important link with his new possessions. Accordingly he called a truce and sent messages to Iorwerth of Caerleon and other leading Welsh insurgents calling upon them to meet him at Newport when he returned from Ireland. He also issued letters of safe-conduct to all those whom he summoned to attend.

The Marcher Lords of the South were furious! Whilst Henry was in word and deed their ruler in respect of their estates in England, in Wales and the Marches his writ carried no force. His attempt to mediate in this war they therefore saw as unwarranted interference that would establish an unwelcome precedent for the future.

It was Earl William who came up with a simple, bloody, and effective solution. His men waylaid and murdered Iorwerth's son Owain on his way to the conference under cover of the King's safe conduct. This graphically illustrated to the Welsh just how much the King's word meant in the Marches, and the violence continued.

Henry clapped his Earl in prison and took possession of Caerleon, the seizure of which from Iorweth had been the principal cause of the uprising in Gwent. With William behind bars Henry tried a second time, on this occasion utilising the good relations he enjoyed with Prince Rhys ap Gryffydd of Deheubarth who with his brother had attacked Aberafan castle in 1153. Amongst the chieftains Rhys brought to meet the King at Gloucester in 1175 to answer for their 'depredations' were Gryffydd the son of Ivor Bach of Senghenydd and Morgan ap Caradoc of Avan. The latter therefore had obviously continued hostilities against the Normans after the sack of Kenfig eight years earlier. Even though there is no record of any attacks upon the town during this period (which is not to say that none occurred), life for the Kenfig burgesses must have been far from easy.

This renewed attempt by the King to play the role of peacemaker in the South Wales Marches sadly went the way of the first. When some Breconshire chieftains returned home from the conference they were invited by William de Breos to a feast in his castle at Abergavenny to celebrate the new accord. At the height of the festivities he then had them all massacred which successfully put an end to Royal meddling in the affairs of the March. Henry's subsequent release of Earl William was virtually an admission that he                    was powerless to deliver any peace agreement in the face of Marcher intransigence.

The viciousness of William towards those Welshmen who were (at least nominally) his subjects but opposed his high-handed and unilateral appropriation of their land, is illustrated by an entry on a roll in the Margam MSS collection (Clark, 1883; Birch, 1897: 158). This also indicates that whilst there may be no mention of any military activity within Glamorgan in contemporary documents, hostilities were still in progress. That the incident found any mention in the Abbey records at all is only due to the fact that the monks

*The Seal of Morgan
ap Caradoc*

wanted to explain the background to their acquisition of land at Resolven in the Neath valley where they subsequently established a grange.

According to their account at some stage during this phase of the war a truce was patched up between Morgan and the Earl by which, as was the custom of the time, the Welshman surrendered to his overlord certain individuals as sureties for his good behaviour.

Amongst these hostages was a certain Canaythen ap Robert ab Einon, and when Morgan broke the truce, Earl William, in a petty and savage act of revenge, had Canaythen's eyes put out.

His role in Canaythen's misfortune seems to have weighed heavily on Morgan's conscience for when the unfortunate man was eventually released he attempted to make some recompense by giving him land at Resolven. Blind as he was, the gift in itself was of little practical value to Canaythen but it gave him the wherewithal to strike a bargain with the monks at Margam. With Morgan's consent he ceded the land to the Abbey in return for being cared for by the community for the remainder of his life. Monks with Welsh names rarely occur in the Margam records as members of its community, so I cannot help but wonder if he is the lay-brother named 'Kenaithur' mentioned as a witness to several Abbey charters either side of the year 1200.

By 1177 Earl William was back in circulation once more, and the unrest in South-East-Wales rumbled on, though the only actual details we have relate to events in Gwent. When the Earl died in 1183 the pot boiled over. In part this may have been because the question of the succession to his estates was the subject of debate - his only son having died in 1166. The Welsh chieftains would have been fully aware of this uncertainty, and with the opposition temporarily leaderless sought to take advantage.

As the late Earl's overlord, responsibility for the defence of Glamorgan fell upon the King, Henry II, and it is thanks to this that, for the first time, we get a clear insight into what was going on in the lordship. This comes not from any written account of the action (which was again all but ignored in contemporary chronicles) but rather from the 'Pipe Rolls' of the Royal Exchequer. These list payments made in connection with the conflict which supplement the bare bones of the brief and enigmatic statement in the Annals of Margam (Luard, 1864) that Kenfig town was burned by the Welsh in 1185 but "had not been burned for a year or more".

By implication the entry infers that there had been a previous attack upon the town which the monastic chronicler had not bothered to include, and this is confirmed by the Pipe Rolls for the year 1183-4. So much damage had been caused to the burgesses' property during this year that the accounts show the rents due upon the burgages was remitted in order to aid the necessary rebuilding work.

This Welsh onslaught was moreover no simple and mindless lashing out at the Norman occupiers but rather a campaign conducted with some forethought and planning. Amongst the other payments made by the Crown in 1183-4 were sums of money devoted to the repair of the river bridges at Rhymny and Roath. These carried the main road into Glamorgan, and their destruction would have hampered Norman reinforcements from England entering the lordship overland. In this it seems to have been effective, for elsewhere there is mention of a payment for transporting Hamo de Valoygnes and his knights by sea in connection with the war.

De Valoygnes seems to have been the person actually entrusted by the King with the task of quelling the rebellion, but amongst those serving under him were several with local connections. These included Walter Lovel of North Cornelly and Reginald FitzSimon who were the constables of the fortresses at Newcastle and Kenfig respectively. Payn de Turberville of Coity and Walter de Lageles of Laleston were also actively engaged in charge of horsemen and foot soldiers employed at the King's expense amongst whom was probably Gilbert Grammus of Marlas, compensated for having his horse killed by the Welsh. The castles at Neath, Kenfig, Newcastle, Rhymney and Newport all suffered damage in this initial assault – mainly to the gates and palisades that formed the outer defences.

In 1185 the second Welsh offensive concentrated upon the three principal towns in the Lordship of Glamorgan – Cardiff, Kenfig, and Neath. Kenfig town, as recorded by the Margam scribe, was again destroyed, but it was at Neath that the main Welsh effort was apparently directed. Here they arrived before the town walls equipped for a regular siege with several 'engines of war' designed to batter down the defences. Once again however De Valognes made good use of the Norman command of the sea to convey his army to the scene of the action and drive off the attackers.

The attacks upon Cardiff and Kenfig were likewise repulsed, but damage had been caused to the outworks of Kenfig castle. Hywel, the son of Iorweth of Caerleon (who had apparently decided that his best chance of regaining that lordship lay in supporting the King) was therefore charged with despatching timber from Chepstow to repair the castle and town walls. Subsequently 24 vessels were chartered for this purpose, and this entry is interesting because it illustrates that whilst the town and garrison were still holding out, the surrounding countryside was too unsafe for them to obtain such supplies locally[24].

There are no further indications of the war continuing beyond 1185. In passing we may note that it was probably during this bout of hostilities that the fratricidal Cadwallon of Glynrhondda met his end leading an assault on an unnamed castle where a wall collapsed upon him. Subsequent records, particularly those of Margam Abbey, show that the Welsh had in fact achieved considerable success during the uprising. I find it significant, for example, that the accounts of 1185 make no mention of repairs to the castle at Newcastle, Bridgend. Had it been ignored during this second phase of the Welsh onslaught—or had it been captured by them? After Prince John (the future King John of Magna Carta fame) took charge of Glamorgan on his marriage to Isabel, daughter of

---

[24] This entry in the Pipe Rolls is also taken as proof of the existence of a port at Kenfig, but I have my doubts. The payment is for the hire of the 24 vessels to convey timber required for the repairs at the castle which is not the same as saying that they were actually carrying it all the way to its destination. It may just as easily have been dropped off at Newton, where there was a far safer harbour, and hauled overland to its destination. (see Appendix II for more on this.)

Earl William in 1189, he actually granted this castle and manor to Morgan ap Caradoc of Avan. As the author of the RCAHMW 1991 report upon this castle states, this was either "an extraordinary gesture of conciliation" or the wily prince was simply acknowledging the status quo which he was powerless to challenge.

This arrangement is in fact in line with the situation that is apparent throughout lowland Glamorgan from Margam charters covering the next thirty years or so[25]. The descendants of Ivor Bach at Senghenydd, for example, apparently acquired the manor of Leckwith (Birch, 1897: 123) where the Pipe Rolls mention the destruction of the corn mill in 1183-4. In the Llancarvan area Morgan ap Caradoc is found in possession of some land known as 'Pultimor' (Pwll Du Mawr) (Birch, 1897: 156) whilst an adjoining holding at Bradington was also in Welsh hands. This last was clearly not to the liking of Henry de Humfraville of Penmark who was the former owner. He was imprisoned for a time by Prince John for some unspecified reason, so perhaps Henry had been unwise enough to press his opposition to John's accommodation with the Welsh a little too vigorously.

The gifts of land at Bradington were confirmed to Margam by both Morgan of Avan and his brother Maredudd of Miskin (Birch, 1897: 124), whilst the latter on his own account also gave the monks the right to take timber from his woods for their grange at Llancarvan. This was made in terms which suggest that these were far closer to this grange than those within his own lordship (Birch, 1897: 161).

It rather seems therefore that Prince John, in order to secure peace in Glamorgan, allowed the Welsh to retain property they had acquired in the lowlands during the course of the war. Such an arrangement would have been typical of the way in which this

---

[25] Almost all these documents are undated, but over many years, through cross-referencing the persons mentioned in them, and by noting the incidence of the properties to which these charters relate in the (dated) charters confirming such gifts to the Abbey, I have been able to work out a rough chronology. (See Appendix V),

complex character from our past operated. He had bigger fish to fry in his quest for the English throne, so he reached an accommodation with Morgan ap Caradoc and the other Welsh chieftains that allowed them to retain the lands they occupied within the lordship.

This created a precarious balance of power within its borders. The Welsh for their part were only too aware that they owed their continued possession of these lands to him, and if they caused further problems John would throw his weight behind the local Anglo-Norman lords to re-take them. The latter were equally aware that if they in turn caused trouble, John would use his native allies against them. They were not enamoured with the situation as the events which followed John's death were to show, but in the meantime they were powerless to take steps to eradicate the Welsh presence on their doorsteps. Rather surprisingly this unstable and uneasy truce was to last for some thirty years, but once John was in his grave it was not long before hostilities broke out afresh.

# Chapter 5

## THE UNEASY TRUCE

Despite the fact that their town had been destroyed by the Welsh twice in just over a year, the castle seriously damaged, and that they were now cut off from the main Anglo-Norman settlement in the Vale, the people of Kenfig clung on. They rebuilt their shattered homes and like business opportunists the world over, set about making a living from the new environment into which fate had cast them. Whether they liked it, or liked it not, they now found themselves living virtually cheek by jowl with the Welsh, and it was an experience I feel may well have shaped the future of the town.

To the east Morgan ap Caradoc controlled the road to Cardiff from his fortress at Newcastle. On the west lay his land of Avan with castles at Aberafan and Baglan. Here he further increased his stranglehold on the highway west and the Norman outpost at Neath by constructing a castle at Briton Ferry (on a hillock that is now beneath the M4 viaduct). This controlled the difficult crossing over the Neath estuary across which Morgan personally escorted Archbishop Baldwin and his entourage in 1188 as described by Giraldus Cambrensis. Perched as it was on a hillock high above a bend in the river the garrison of this castle could also have challenged vessels seeking to proceed upstream to Neath town and castle. Whilst Morgan had been unable to capture either of the fortresses at Kenfig and Neath or their associated towns, he now effectively controlled access to both.

In the case of Kenfig, Morgan could also count upon the support of the Welsh community at Tir Iarll in the hills to the north, so the borough was indeed surrounded on all sides. The Welsh had even encroached onto the lands of Kenfig Territory itself. It is at this time that we begin to hear mention in the Margam charters of "the lands of the free Welshmen" virtually in sight of the town walls.

Not to put too fine a point upon it relations between the two communities – the Welsh and the Anglo-Normans – had not been good. Earl William of Gloucester, as we have seen, had not been alone in treating the native population and their rulers with contempt. Treaties had been broken, land seized, murder and atrocities committed upon the Welsh with impunity, and with little apparent justification. Significantly, English sources of the time neither mention nor claim similar acts against the Norman population, but we can well imagine that the contempt of the invaders was returned with interest. It has always seemed to me that here in Wales in the late 12th and early 13th century we had a precursor of the situation that arose in America between the white settlers and the native Indian tribes. The only thing missing were the firearms!

Locally, new Anglo-Norman defences were constructed in stone at the castles of Ogmore and Coity, and the first substantial fortifications also appeared at Ewenny Priory. In response, Morgan seems to have strengthened his own fortress at Newcastle[26] tightening his grip on this key point on the main coastal highway.

The reaction of the people of the Borough of Kenfig to these developments can best be gauged by studying the response of the Anglo-Norman population in the settlements beyond its walls. They

---

[26] The Royal Commission report on this fortress tends to dismiss a Welsh origin for this castle on the rather dubious grounds that its defences are more substantial than those of Morgan's existing fortress at Baglan. This ignores the fact that the latter was not at this time in 'the front line', and that in the case of Newcastle Morgan would have been able to draw upon masons already engaged on work at Coity, Ogmore and Ewenny. To me it has always been significant that the main entrance to the fort at Newcastle is a very simple gateway in the wall with none of the defences apparent at other contemporary castles in the area. This is also the case at Castell Morgraig, north of Cardiff which is another (slightly later) fortress that is also believed to be of Welsh origin. Significantly the same is also true of the gateway of Dolforwyn castle built by Prince Llywelyn ap Gryffydd in 1273 (Lawrence Butler, 'Dolforwyn Castle', *Current Archaeology* No 197 (2005), pp 296-234). Such plain, simple gateways therefore seem to have been a feature of Welsh castles even a century later.

were even more vulnerable to attack than their countrymen within the town and some, like the Sturmy family, had elected to get out even before a peace was patched up.

### The Sturmies of Stormy

Stormy manor had been given to Geoffrey Sturmy (whose family hailed from Wiltshire) sometime prior to the year 1154[27]. He then constructed a village, a chapel and castle on the north side of Stormy Down the name of which stems from this family and has nothing whatsoever to do with the weather! Towards the end of his life Geoffrey became infirm and entered Margam monastery as a lay-brother in fulfilment of an undertaking made by the monks as part of a deal whereby he granted them some of his land on the south slope of Cefn Cribwr ridge. He was obviously also in financial difficulties at this time and things did not improve for his son and heir Roger. Whilst his father was still alive the two of them jointly gave the Abbey another slice of the manor bordering what is today Waunbant Road, Kenfig Hill in return for a further donation to help them settle their debts.

None of the Sturmy charters are dated, but this was possibly about the time that war broke out with the sack of Kenfig in 1167. Roger, his family and their villagers could take shelter in the keep of their castle when danger threatened, the entry to the tower that formerly crowned the motte would have been on the first floor and reached by a ladder. As there is no indication of an outer ward or bailey at the location today there was no way they could protect their cattle, sheep and other livestock, far less any crops growing in the fields.

As the family's situation grew ever more precarious Roger arrived at a solution. The remainder of his land in the manor was split into two halves. One he rented to a Welshman called Gryffydd

---

[27] For a fuller explanation of the origins and history of the Sturmy family see my (1990 unpublished) book *'Sturmi's Land'* available at local Bridgend libraries.

Vychan on the latter's marriage to his daughter (Alice Sturmy). That such a union was brought about by necessity rather than choice is indicated by the fact that (rather like Earl William's settlement with Margam Abbey) the actual grant was made by Roger's son and heir Roger junior and he merely gave his assent. This land later became the manor of Horgrove (modern Haregrove).

The other half Roger gave to the monks of Margam in return for the annulment of certain debts and some 'gifts' that included "three cows to provide milk for the babies", his own cattle having presumably been carried off by the Welsh. Similarly his wife Gunnilda received (amongst other gifts) a flock of twenty sheep in return for her dower land which lay on the slope below Pencastell Farm on Cefn Cribwr ridge. This property transfer did not, however, amount to a sale of the property, for all Roger did at this stage was to rent this half of his land to the monks for £5 per annum which clearly allowed him the option to return at a later date. He had, however, reckoned without the monks!

Although initially impressed by the work of the Cistercians at Margam on the occasion of his visit there in 1188, towards the end of his life Giraldus Cambrensis became highly critical of the way in which the Order operated in his native country. Professor F G Cowley (1977) identifies one story he told to illustrate their methods of acquiring land concerning an (unnamed) Welsh manor that he equated with Llangewydd near Laleston. Whether or not this is the case, the story could just as equally be applied to Stormy.

Having acquired the manor the monks immediately demolished the castle, reasoning that without it, the owner would find returning there very difficult! One thinks immediately of the deliberate filling-in of the ditch around the motte at Stormy, though in truth this may have been done at a later date. They then demolished the village church in a single night, and hid the demolition material so that it could not be re-assembled. This they did to encourage the villagers to move away, for the rules of their Order did not permit the monks to live off the labour of others.

Again the location that I believe to be that of the church at Stormy is a platform site orientated East-West, but utterly devoid of the trace of any building upon it.

There are indications that the villagers whom Roger Sturmy had rather callously abandoned to the tender mercies of the monks took refuge with his son-in-law Gryffydd Vychan who allowed them to create a new settlement that by the end of the century had become known as Horgrove (modern Haregrove). One way or the other, we know that by the year 1177 at the very latest the Sturmies had gone. They may perhaps have been the first, but they were certainly not the last!

## Hugh de Hereford

Once it became apparent that the Welsh were here to stay (at least for the foreseeable future) others followed the Sturmies' lead. In the case of Hugh de Hereford the series of deals he concluded with the Abbot of Margam may in part have been prompted by problems other than the proximity of his new Welsh neighbours. Earl William of Gloucester had apparently given Hugh this land in gratitude for service he had performed at an unnamed castle for forty days presumably during the unrest following the sack of Kenfig in 1167.

From Hugh's own charters it is difficult to work out exactly where his land lay. One of the earliest (Birch, 1897: 60-1) which can be dated to the period 1174-83 speaks of it lying 'in Margam' which in the later documents becomes 'Kenfig Territory'. In all it amounted to 100 acres (Birch, 1897: 178) and bordered both Walter Lupellus's manor at North Cornelly and some of the 'Welsh Lands'. Hugh owed some sort of service to the Earl for this holding but it is nowhere specified what this was.

During my research into the origins of Stormy Grange however I did discover one vital clue which enabled me to say that part (perhaps all) of Hugh's land lay along the south side of the Avan Fach to the south of Pyle (Griffiths, 1990: 46). This in turn suggested that "the highway coming from the chapel of Corneli belonging to Walter Lupellus towards the water" mentioned in these charters is probably the road from North Cornelly to the ford called Redesice across the Afan Fach at Pyle[28]. This therefore gives us a rough idea of where Hugh's land was, indicating that it extended from this road up Stormy Down along the line of the A48. I have often wondered if it was he who perhaps established the first farmstead at Ty Draw (now buried beneath the traffic roundabout).

A later charter tells of how some time after his initial grant to the Abbey, Hugh was imprisoned by Earl William and had to find nine silver marks to secure his release (Birch, 1897: 60). He raised the money from the abbot by mortgaging 'all his land upon Cornelly', but his difficulties did not end there. Further 'grants' (that are in effect bills of sale) followed, so that by 1203 and despite opposition from members of his family, all Hugh's property had passed to the Abbey.

## Thomas Lageles

I have surmised that Hugh de Hereford's difficulties may have been caused in part by the proximity of his land to those of the Welsh, but at Laleston Thomas Lageles was in an even worse position. He is presumably the son of Walter Lageles who like Hugh had been involved in the war against the Welsh, but his land at Laleston was a sub-manor of Newcastle which of course was now in the hands of Morgan ap Caradoc. Thomas was therefore required to perform service to the Welshman and pay him 8s 6d a year annual rent.

Sometime between 1186 and 1203 he gave to the monks all his demesne land (i.e. the land he himself actually owned as opposed to that of his serfs and tenants) and retired to the Abbey as a lay-brother (Birch, 1897: 152). He then followed this with the gift of

---

[28] Now marked by the bridge giving access to the Crown Inn and Orchard Cottage. Interpreted in this manner the entry also tends to suggest that the Chapel of St Wenduin at North Cornelly (the location of which is otherwise unknown) was possibly the first building on this road as it entered that village.

all his land which was confirmed by his overlord Morgan ap Caradoc in 1205.

### David Scurlage

The Scurlages held the manor of Llangewydd (north of Laleston) from the lord of Glamorgan by virtue of knight service and had been generous donors to the Abbey prior to 1186, but in 1202 David Scurlage rented his manor to the monks (Birch, 1897: 149) in similar fashion to Roger Sturmy. The result here was virtually identical, for his family was also fated never to return. As with Hugh de Hereford the disposal of this land was opposed from within David's family, specifically by his illegitimate brother Raymond and a Nicholas Puinz. They appear to have claimed that David was still a minor when he made the agreement though this was subsequently disproved at the County Court.

What the relationship was between Nicholas and David Scurlage is nowhere stated, but his claim was apparently sufficiently strong for the Abbot to pay him generous expenses towards the cost of the litigation and subsequently secured from him a document renouncing his claim. Indeed, in subsequent charters confirming the various gifts of property to the Abbey, Nicholas's name appears with David's as a party to the agreement in respect of Llangewydd.

### Gilbert Grammus and those who stayed

Roger Sturmy, Hugh de Hereford, Thomas Lageles and David Scurlage were four major landholders in the former territory of Morgan who opted to leave the district rather than remain in the face of the Welsh presence. Others, however, chose to stay and 'tough it out'. Perhaps the most interesting of these are the Grammus family who probably lived at Marlas which was certainly their home later in the 13th century. A Gilbert Grammus had been actively engaged in the recent conflict, his horse being killed in the fighting that broke out immediately following Earl William's death.

Despite this they seem to have been able to achieve some sort of accommodation with the new arrivals.

Gilbert is possibly the same man who gave Margam 10 acres of land near the 'old cemetery' at Kenfig in a deed that can be shown to date to the year 1203 (Birch, 1897: 157). The previous year Phillip Grammus 'the Elder' (who was perhaps Gilbert's son) had leased ten acres to Margam Abbey, and interestingly the transaction was carried out 'according to Welsh custom' (Birch, 1897: 184). Another Phillip Grammus current at this time was probably Gilbert's grandson of that name who subsequently confirmed his grandfather's gift. Other contemporary documents refer to a 'Gille' Grammus who is obviously Gilbert himself and he is probably identical with a 'Gille Seis' mentioned in other Abbey charters involving a grant of land by him 'in Kenfig' (Birch, 1897: 167). 'Gille' (as we have noted in the case of 'Gillemichel') seems to be a Welsh rendering of 'Gilbert', so he achieved sufficiently good relations with the Welsh neighbours to at least have acquired a nickname from them!

This also seems to have been the case with another Anglo-Norman named Joaf who held land near Catteputte (Pwllygath, Kenfig Hill) and is referred to in one document (Birch, 1897: 236) as Joaf 'Troinkam' (Trwyn Cam – Bent nose).

The Lovels and the De Cornelly family also seem to have continued through the years of Welsh occupation unscathed. In the case of the latter the occurrence of a 'Wronu' (Gronow) de Cornelly as witness to a charter in the first half of the 13th century may hint at a marriage alliance with the interlopers.

Others who fall into this category are the sons of Gillemichel and the sons of Herbert mentioned in an earlier chapter. They seem to have thrown their lot in with Morgan ap Caradoc and the 'Herberts' acquired some land on the west of the road from Laleston to Cefn Cribwr whilst the 'Gillemichels' are mentioned at Pencastell ('Castle Kibbur'). These intermarriages seem to have worked both ways. Griffith Vychan, it will be remembered, married Alice Sturmy as part of her father's settlement on his departure from the district. Their children bore a mixture of Welsh and English names and adopted 'Vychan' in the anglicised form 'Began' as a surname. They also seem to have created a typical feudal settlement at the village of Horgrove, perhaps for those serfs driven out of Sturmiestown by the monks. Whilst the Herberts and the Gillemichels became Welsh, the Begans became English and there is some evidence that they were the originators of a family of Cardiff burgesses of this name.

Beyond the walls of Kenfig therefore the Anglo-Norman settlers of the district reacted to the Welsh re-settlement of the district in a variety of ways. Some left, but those who remained nevertheless found it possible to live in harmony cheek by jowl with 'the enemy'. One would expect therefore to find similar reactions amongst the Kenfig Burgesses, and there are indeed some pointers that this was the case.

In this connection two of the Kenfig Ordinances in particular are worthy of mention though we cannot say when exactly they were made other than it was prior to the creation of Cowbridge Borough circa 1249-54[29]. Both speak of a time when there was apparent paranoia about the security of the town though, in truth, the burgesses always seem to have harboured a certain antipathy towards 'outsiders' generally. They may therefore pre-date the Welsh occupation, but their existence is still of interest.

The first of these (Number 25) is perhaps one of the most curious in the entire roll. It forbade all burgesses and chencers (persons engaged in business who were not burgesses) to "goe out of the franchise and libertys of the said town to the wedding ale of any person or persons whatsoever". A 'wedding ale' was a function held by the family of the happy couple who brewed up a large quantity of drink that was freely available to anyone who wished to attend provided they brought a gift to enable the newly-weds to set up home. This therefore seems to be one of those bye-laws added to

---

[29] See Appendix V for the evidence about the dates of Charters and Ordinances.

the Kenfig roll in the light of previous experience. 'When the beer is in, common sense goes out' (as they say!), and given the general antipathy between town and country may have led to outbreaks of violence even without the Welsh presence. At the same time following the implementation of Prince John's peace settlement in 1211 the Corporation may have been concerned that their new neighbours might use or even engineer such an event to capture any burgesses attending and hold them hostage.

The other bye-law (No 35) declares that "noe stranger shall walke by night after nine of the clock without a reasonable cause, or fire in his hand". A 'stranger' was anyone who was not a resident so the law reflects the burgesses' aversion to any outsiders skulking round their town in the dark.

Undoubtedly too some burgesses will have followed the example set by the Sturmies and simply abandoned the place to seek a better (and quieter!) life elsewhere. G.T.Clarke (1883: 57) found that a hundred or so families from Glamorgan either participated in the invasion of Ireland in 1169-71 or settled there soon afterwards. Amongst them was a family that adopted the surname De Chenefeg[30] whose descendants still survive today using the same surname, though in a variety of forms.

So like their countrymen outside the walls many within the town apparently found it difficult to accept the Welsh occupation of the surrounding countryside, but did those who remained also emulate the Grammus family and seek an accommodation with their new neighbours? There is some evidence that suggests they did.

Later in Kenfig's history, leather working seems to have been the dominant industry within the town – sufficiently important for the cordwainers (shoemakers) and glovers to form themselves

---

[30] These families seem to have originated from an area east of Cork, and have variations of the surname Kenefig which is the name of the town in the earliest documents in which it is mentioned. There are also two location in East Cork called Bally*kenefick* and Garrane*kenefeake* respectively

into a craft guild. That being the case, where did they acquire the animal hides to be turned into leather? The cattle pastured by the burgesses of Kenfig on their common seem to have been dairy cows kept solely for their milk. When, indeed, an attempt was made to introduce young cattle onto these pastures, the Corporation apparently moved to stamp it out (Ordinance No 48).

Beyond the Borough in the outlying settlements the idea of rearing cattle for such a trade is unlikely to have found much favour hitherto because of the likelihood of Welsh raids. Like the burgesses the serfs and tenants on the manors kept sufficient cows only to meet their needs for butter and cheese. Rearing cattle and sheep in the agriculturally poor land of the Blaenau was nevertheless part of the Welsh way of life. From them the tanners at Kenfig would have been able to secure a steady supply of skins and hides establishing an economic link between the communities that continued even after the Welsh settlers were forced to abandon their land near the town.

### Cordwainers & Glovers

It is interesting also that the bye-laws relating to the trade in hides and leather occur quite late in the series of Ordinances, but certainly before 1254. Number 40 requires tanners to sell only leather that was "well and sufficiently tanned" whilst the purchase of "hides or skinns of any beasts or cattle whatsoever, or wool" could only be made "in the common markett place of old accustomed" (no 41). These are followed by another requiring that meat offered for sale in the market be of good quality and "strange butchers" (were allowed to trade on Fridays and Saturdays only) who brought it there also had to bring the skins and hides of the animals with them. This was probably nothing to do with promoting the leather trade but rather a measure designed to stamp out rustling. No laws were necessary to regulate the standard of the work of the shoemakers and glovers as these were imposed and enforced by their own guild — the Cordwainers & Glovers.

The name of this guild (the only one in Kenfig) with its implicit amalgamation of two groups of craftsmen working in leather reflects the manner in which the medieval period perceived the work of the industry, each group involved having their own distinctive methods[31]. They produced an end-product from raw material provided by tanners, curriers and tawyers who processed the skins of animals such as cattle, pigs, horses and sheep to turn it into leather, a process that had changed but little from the days of the Romans.

The process started with the butchers of Kenfig who (to judge by the Ordinances) were a pretty unruly bunch! As well as Ordinance No 42 relating to the quality of meat sold in the market with its restrictions upon 'strange butchers', three out of the first eleven bye-laws were designed to keep the activities of the resident butchers in check. They were not to sell meat on Sundays nor kill animals and process meat in the High Street, and none were to deposit "noe heads, feet nor none other garbage" either there or elsewhere in the town "to the annoyance of his neighbour". Their activities were, in fact, restricted to The Shambles, a street found in most medieval towns the very name of which has become a bye-word for the chaos that normally ruled there as terrified animals were slaughtered and their meat processed on and alongside the thoroughfare.

Having removed from the carcass all that was profitable, the butcher sold the hide (with horns, legs and hooves still attached) to the tanner who first trimmed off these appendages and washed it clean – often by immersing it for a time in a nearby stream or river.

The next task was to rid the skin of hair which initially involved allowing as much as possible to rot away, a process that was sometimes encouraged by sprinkling the hides with urine or soaking them in a solution of lime or wood ash. Tanning, it has to be

---

[31] Much of what follows is based on Cherry, John *Leather* in Blair & Ramsey eds. (1991: 295-318) *English Medieval Industries*.

said was a very, very smelly business! Having been scraped to remove all vestiges of hair and flesh the hides were next immersed in a warm solution made with bird droppings or dog dung to remove the lime and give them a softer and more flexible texture. Another part of this process involved solutions made with fermented barley, stale beer, and urine - our medieval forebears having got 'recycling' down to a very fine art!

Once the hides had again been thoroughly washed, the process of tanning could actually begin. This involved immersing them in a weak tanning solution and moving them around daily to ensure that the colour was uniform across the surface. Finally the hides were removed to pits of water in which they were laid down between layers of vegetable tanning material (usually oak bark) where they remained for at least a twelve-month before being placed in a dark, airy building to dry.

The tanners worked mainly with cattle hides and used oak in the process but tawyers processed other skins (such as sheep, pig and horse) using alum and oil in the process. There is no specific mention of them at Kenfig, but the softer leathers they produced were the type used by glovers. Also, unlike the tanners, the tawyers seem to have completed the entire process of preparing the skins ready for use by the craftsmen whereas leather produced in the tanneries was then sold on to curriers. These rendered the material supple by soaking, pummelling and trampling, stretching and paring it down to an uniform thickness before working into the leather a dubbin made of tallow and fish oils. Firm leather for the soles of shoes or horse harness was then allowed to dry and season and finally the surface dyed or polished using a flat stone.

Leather making was therefore a long process that involved several trades even before the final product reached the hands of the craftsmen who would turn it into shoes, harness, gloves and clothing. Needless to say therefore the end-products tended to be expensive!

The Kenfig Cordwainers would have produced their shoes by the 'turnshoe' method where the uppers were stitched onto the soles (flax usually being used as the thread) and the whole then turned inside-out. In some cases soles were made of wood beneath which an iron ring called a pattern was often fitted to raise the footwear above the layer of mud (and other things!) that normally carpeted medieval streets.

Exactly how extensive the Kenfig leather-trade was is impossible to say, though the tanneries in particular would show up in excavation from the various pits used in the process. The documentary evidence however points to the trade having been an important – perhaps the most important – industry in the town, and may well have owed its origin to the period at the end of the 12th century when the Welsh were living in the immediate vicinity.

In their various ways therefore the Anglo-Norman settlers that chose to remain in and around Kenfig attempted to forge a new relationship with the Welsh who had suddenly been catapulted into their midst. Friendships may even have developed from business contacts between individuals, and certainly there was inter-marriage, but the underlying enmity between the two races would take a lot longer to evaporate.

# Chapter 6

## THE LANDS OF THE FREE WELSHMEN

If many of the Anglo-Norman settlers found difficulty in accepting the presence of the Welsh in the territory between the Ogmore and Kenfig rivers, those on the other side of the ethnic divide were also uneasy about their situation. Several realised right from the outset that their occupation of this land was likely to be temporary and others came to share their view when John (now King of England) divorced his wife Isabel in 1199.

      She was one of three daughters of the late Earl William of Gloucester and who, there being no surviving son, by rights should have shared her father's estates with her sisters. In fact she inherited them virtually intact. This was because it was claimed that the Earl had adopted John as his legal heir provided that he married Isabel. If the explanation lacks credibility today, let me assure you that there were many who thought the same at the time! Nevertheless when the marriage was finally celebrated in 1189 John took sole charge of the former Gloucester estates in England and Wales. It was not a happy union, and more importantly failed to produce an heir and hence the divorce ten years later.

      By rights John should have restored Isabel's estates to her there and then, but he had never been a stickler for observing laws that were inconvenient to him personally! He may well have touted his alleged adoption by Earl William as justification; after all—he had married Isabel hadn't he? So instead he retained Gloucester's estates and treated them as his own. Glamorgan's Welsh leaders were not, however, to know this. The law as they understood it stated that Isabel would become their new overlord and they had little doubt they could expect little sympathy from the daughter of

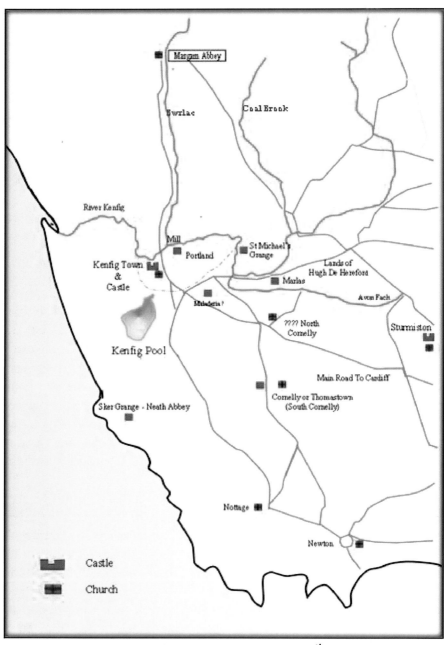

*Map 3: Kenfig & District in the late 12th Century*

their late and un-lamented overlord. Nor was there any comfort to be drawn from the fact that her late husband kept control of the estates. Isabel had not borne him any children, and she (since the fault was clearly not John's who had several illegitimate offspring) was unlikely to do so in the event of his allowing her to remarry. It would not have taken them long therefore to work out that her successor would be her nephew Gilbert de Clare, a Marcher Baron cast from the same mould as William of Gloucester. The good times were drawing to a close, and each Welsh tenant prepared to face the future in his own way.

For many this meant cashing in all or part of their assets in the lowlands. They were the clever ones, bartering their land to the Abbey at Margam in return for money. Others were (or thought they were) a little more cunning, renting their property to the monks in the same manner as Roger Sturmy and David Scurlage. Whatever the future, they reasoned, what Anglo-Norman lord would have the temerity to interfere with a sacred bond entered into with God's chosen? Such behaviour would bring down the wrath of the Church with its 'bell, book and candle' about his ears. Meanwhile all they had to do was collect the annual rent.

In 1203 Pope Innocent III issued a Papal Bull to the Abbey at Margam confirming to it all gifts of land and privileges granted up to that time. On it are listed some of the more important 'gifts' of land made by Welshmen in the Kenfig district and also, for the first time, smaller 'bequests' from others lumped together under the heading 'the free Welshmen of Kenfig'.

That same year, following some sort of internal investigation by the Cistercian Order, Abbot Roger was dismissed from office at the Abbey for unspecified reasons. I often wonder if those appointed to the task saw all too plainly what he clearly had not – that the acquisition of this property would inevitably draw the community itself into the looming dispute between the Welsh and a future Lord of Cardiff castle. The Cistercians, however, were renowned for the manner in which they acquired land, so whilst the perpetrator was punished for his action, no attempt was apparently made to stave off the crisis by reversing the process!

From the various charters in the former archives of the Abbey it is possible to work out roughly where some of this Welsh territory in Kenfig lay, though in truth the term seems to have included some who were of Anglo-Norman descent. I will spare general readers the details of how I worked out the location of these lands by keeping my account brief and utilising footnotes. Basically however they seem to have adjoined the two main roads leading east from the borough – the ancient trackway running up onto Cefn Cribwr ridge via the later villages of Pyle and Kenfig Hill; and the main highway to Cardiff. The latter, known as The Portway, ran from the town along a different route than that followed by the later A48 trunk road. From Cornelly Cross it climbed the slopes of Cornelly Down (now Stormy Down) along the lane known as Heol y Sheet, and then continued to the ford across the Ogmore River at Bridgend via Laleston and the fortress of Newcastle in Bridgend.

### The Peitevin Land
The first piece of identifiable 'Welsh Land' on the main highway lay at Cornelly Cross in the angle between Heol-y-Sheet and the road leading to South Cornelly. A certain Ketherech the son of John Du gave Margam Abbey two plots of land here in separate grants (Birch, 1897: 30) that can be fairly closely dated to the period 1186 to 1189. The first of these was for five acres "of his free tenement in the land of Peithuin", and the second for a further fifteen "in Peituin" adjoining them. Identifying this property gave me particular pleasure as its location has long puzzled local historians; some of them had identified it with Pyle on nothing more than a vague similarity in the names[32].

---

[32] The five acres in the first grant lay "near the highway which leads from Kenefec towards Cardiff, along the vill of Walter Lupellus". This 'vill' was North Cornelly which lay on the opposite side of Heol y Sheet to the land I have identified along a side track which led from it towards Pyle.

It was, in fact, the early name for Tytanglwyst which is first mentioned as 'Tanguestellond' in a document dating to the latter half of the 13th century (Birch, 1897: 141). How it got this name is uncertain. The current fashion is to identify it as 'Ty dan yr Eglwys' (The house below the church) which is rather unsatisfactory in that the nearest church is the chapel at South Cornelly which is actually 'below the house'! The earliest form of the name suggests instead that the present one derives from 'Tir Tanglwyst' (Tanglwyst's Land) and 'Tanguistel' was actually the name of Ketherech's wife.

I know nothing of Ketherech's father John Du, but there were at least two other sons – Caradoc Du and Kenaithur. Ketherech's only child was a daughter named Thatherech who married Iorwerth ap Gistelard of Catteputte (Pwllygath, Kenfig Hill) member of another Anglo-Norman family apparently in the process of 'going native'. In 1197 Thatherech leased the Peitevin land to the monks for a half a silver mark a year with six year's rent paid beforehand (Birch, 1897: 142). On her death the rent was to reduce to four shillings "for her soul" a deal that probably meant that masses would be said for her well-being in the hereafter. Her deed is followed by quit-claims

*Heol y Sheet descending*
*Stormy Down towards*
*North Cornelly and Mawdlam*

from her husband and sons of their rights to the property.

This was not all the Peitevin land however, as some of it seems to have passed from Ketherech to his nephew Espus Du, the son of his brother Caradoc. By 1207 he had let part of it together with seven acres his father had held in Cornelly to the Abbey at the nominal rent of two spurs or sixpence annually (Birch, 1897: 162-3). Shortly afterwards he added the remainder at a consolidated rent of half a mark annually with the curious proviso that if he died without an heir the Abbey was to have the land but otherwise the monks were to have just twelve acres and the rent reduced by two shillings. Whatever the result the Abbot undertook to ensure Espus's body was buried in the Abbey precincts (Birch, 1897: 162). From the information contained in these charters and others it is possible to work out that the land Ketherech had held amounted to roughly a hundred acres (about 68 in modern measure).

## Ballas

Further along the Cardiff road towards the summit there was also some Welsh presence at Ballas – a name that seems to derive from the so-called 'Danish Camp' which was actually a prehistoric livestock corral of which no trace now remains[33]. In 1219 Gronow Bil made a grant to the monks that included five acres which lay "beginning at a places called Balles and reaching towards Goylake" (the Avan Fach) (Birch, 1897: 216).

Even more interestingly a group of Welshmen sold eleven acres of land "in Kenefeg manor at Balles" to William Alexander about the middle of the 13th century (PM 1969). This was after Gilbert de Clare had apparently driven the Welsh out of the Kenfig lowlands. I suspect therefore that their ancestors may have actually

---

[33] A rough plan was included by Frederick Evans in his 1912 book *Tir Iarll* (p.36). It lay in the angle between Heol-y-Sheet and the A 48 road, and it is likely that the circular body of the earthwork gave the place its name. So far as I am aware its age was never tested by excavation, but Leslie Evans (1964, *The Story of Kenfig* ) records that a cairn lying between it and the road belonged to the early Bronze Age.

been tenants of one of the Cornelly manors as was the case with Espus Du who owned seven acres within the manor of North Cornelly as mentioned above. Here again we may have a clue as to how the Lovel and De Cornelly families arrived at some sort of accommodation with the Welsh during the uneasy peace engineered by Prince (later King) John.

## Cadwgan's Land

This was a block of land that later formed the basis of Parcau Isaf Farm (now a private house) on the north side of the main road beyond Stormy Down towards Laleston. It lay in the north-west angle of a crossroads formed where the main highway was intersected by another road leading from Tythegston to Cefn Cribwr. Today this is marked by a roundabout, though the northern extension of the Tythegston Road (formerly known as Heol Twmshill) has long been abandoned.

Amongst the local Police and Traffic Officers this location was generally known as Redhill Roundabout from a farm that formerly existed here, but this name seems not to have been used by the general public who normally call it simply 'the Porthcawl Roundabout'. In those times it was known as 'Walter's Cross', perhaps a reference to Walter Lageles one of the lords of nearby Laleston.

From the main road Cadwgan's Land stretched north to the summit of the down where an earth bank marked the boundary with the lands of Horgrove. After being acquired by the monks they extended this land westwards along the main road, and subsequently this extension became Parcau Uchaf Farm.

The name 'Parcau' (Park) applied to the two farms that evolved from Cadwgan's Land suggests that under the monks the combined area of the two farms formed one large open enclosure. This seemed to be confirmed when I field-walked the area as part of my Stormy project for none of the internal field boundaries appeared to date from the medieval period though interestingly I discovered that a small portion of the enclosure had been devoted to woodland.

Cadwgan's Land takes its name from the sons of Cadwgan who granted it to the Abbey in three documents (Birch, 1897: 66. 145) that can be dated very closely to the years 1202-3, but implicit in these documents is the fact that previously the land had been owned by their father.

## Pencastell

The other major Welsh landholding in the Kenfig district was that of the Anglo-Welsh sons of Gillemichel – William and Cadrawd. The two appear together as sureties in an early deed (pre-1183) from the Margam collection (Birch, 1897: 26-7) and Cadrawd's sons (Gryffydd and Cadrawd) subsequently granted to the Abbey all his former land that lay "beyond Kenefeg[34], near the land of Roger Sturmi" (PM 1965). This deed, unfortunately, is virtually impossible to date.

We know rather more about Cadrawd's brother William who sometimes appears under the name of William Gille or Kille, and is a frequent witness to local deeds and charters towards the end of the 12th century. For his own part he gave the monks eight acres of land in Kenfig "adjacent to the land of Mehi, on the east, in the vicinity of the high road towards Kenfig from Sturmi". Taking this charter in conjunction with information contained in others issued by his descendants I eventually determined that this 'high road' is today Waunbant Road, Kenfig Hill, and that William's charter dates from the period 1187-1203.

Between 1199 and 1203 William's son Walawet added 6½ acres adjoining these (Birch, 1897: 32), together with another acre and a half for the sum of forty shillings (£2). Then (and again before 1203) he gave the monks (Birch, 1897: 33) all his father's land in Kenfig, undertaking to pay "the charges thereof due to the Earl's

---

[34] I take this to be Kenfig river, and the entry to mean that the land was 'beyond' this from the point of view of the Abbey.

kitchen" out of his land of Ketlia'lanwar (Gelli Lenor near Llangynwyd). The Bull confirming the possessions of Margam Abbey issued by Pope Innocent III in 1203 indicates that in all this land amounted to forty acres. Ivor Vychan, who seems to have been another of William's children, ceded his claim to twelve acres of this land which lay in the area now occupied by the Cynffig Comprehensive School (Birch, 1897: 143)

These were the main Welsh landholdings in the area between the rivers Kenfig and Ogmore, but there were other plots that I have so far failed to identify. Taken in conjunction with the Welsh presence at Newcastle the existence of so many Welsh properties adjoining the main road to Cardiff must have left the burgesses of Kenfig feeling rather isolated from the main body of their countrymen in The Vale. Whilst the peace held the road remained open, but what might happen if eventually hostilities broke out anew? That was a topic that must have greatly exercised the thoughts and deliberations of the good burghers when they met together in alehouse and council chamber!

***Remains of the Cloisters at Margam Abbey***

*(from an engraving by Gatineau, 1840)*

# Chapter 7

## HOSTILITIES RENEWED

Rather surprisingly, the fragile peace imposed upon the Welsh and the Anglo-Normans in Glamorgan lasted for over 30 years. That this was so was due almost exclusively to King John who after their divorce clung on to Isabel's estates contrary to all feudal law and practice. As towards the end of his reign his hold on the country crumbled so the prospect of renewed hostilities in Glamorgan drew ever closer.

On January the 26th, 1214 King John, with rather bad grace, allowed his former wife to marry Geoffrey de Mandeville, the Earl of Essex to whom he then transferred the bulk of the Gloucester estates (including Glamorgan). John himself retained the town and castle at Bristol, and imposed a condition whereby those to whom he had granted offices and lands would be allowed to retain them (Painter, 1966: 238). This clause ensured that the Welsh of Glamorgan retained a hold on their estates in the Vale and around Kenfig a little longer, but John's fortunes were in decline and it was just over a twelvemonth later that he was obliged to affix his seal to the Magna Carta.

The affair at Runnymede was, however, but a brief truce in the running battle between King John and his barons. Once he had regained power, the King got the charter annulled by the Pope. The civil war was then renewed with Mandeville throwing in his lot with the baronial party. He would nevertheless have been unwilling to break the terms of the marriage agreement he had concluded with John by ejecting the Glamorgan Welsh from their holdings. To do so would have meant war in South Wales at a time when he and his fellow barons were already struggling to survive against John's determined offensive in England. Again the faltering peace in Glamorgan continued a little longer, but events were now gathering pace.

The death of the Earl of Essex in March 1216 was followed by that of John himself in October, bringing the civil war to an end and leaving the way clear for Isabel to address affairs on her lands in South Wales. She married Hubert de Burgh who was himself a Marcher baron. But before any steps could be taken against the Welsh she herself died in October 1217 and the estate passed to her nephew Gilbert de Clare.

Earl Gilbert is believed to have taken possession of the Gloucester lands sometime in 1218, and within a few years had ejected the Welsh from all their possessions in                    the lowlands—the Kenfig lands and Newcastle manor included. His solution to the potentially thorny question of the property they had rented or donated to the Abbot of Margam was quite novel. He simply took possession of all the land they had acquired in the lowlands, then re-donated the Welsh bequests to the monks – rent free! Not only had he not antagonised the church, he now secured the Abbey's support, and at virtually no cost to himself.

*Seal of Gilbert de Clare*

His actions are apparent from two remarkable charters in the Margam manuscript collection (PM 2046 & 205) whereby Gilbert gave to the Abbey much of the land it had formerly leased from the Welsh in Newcastle and Kenfig as though it was his own. This included a moor called Redes (which is the land upon which Cynffig

Comprehensive school now stands); land near Catteputte; and, rather surprisingly, the land of Horgrove. As related previously this last had been acquired by Gryffydd Began quite legally through his marriage to Alice Sturmy. Closer examination of a series of Abbey charters suggests that Gilbert's gift of their land to the monks may actually have been a further sop to them to ensure their support

A Bull issued in favour of the Abbey by Pope Urban III in 1186 confirmed to the community all lands granted to it up to that point in time. These are listed in some detail, but the Sturmy properties are conspicuous only by their absence despite the fact that all had been made prior to the year 1177 at the very latest. The clue as to what had happened seems to lie in other Margam charters dating from 1234. These indicate that the sons of Gryffydd and Alice challenged the monks' possession of the Sturmy lands, claiming that the rent due upon them should be paid to them, and not their Uncle Roger (as it actually should have been). The absence of Stormy from the Papal Bull perhaps indicates that when the Abbot refused to accede to their demand the Begans took advantage of the Welsh ascendancy in the district to repossess their portion of the former Sturmy manor.

Legal challenges no doubt followed, but whilst 'the land of Sturmi' was confirmed to Margam in the Bull of Pope Innocent III in 1203, it is again omitted from a confirmation charter by King John just two years later. He apparently then took another two years to mull over the situation before issuing a second charter in 1207 confirming all the Sturmy grants. That really should have been the end of the matter, but the sons of Gryffydd Began refused to accept the situation until finally admitting their duplicity in 1234.

When Earl Gilbert became ruler of Glamorgan the Begans were still attempting to force the monks to pay them rent. It may be this that prompted him to take Horgrove (modern Haregrove) out of the family's hands[35] and give it to the Abbey. Whatever the reason, remove it he did, but despite repeated references to Horgrove by historians thereafter as a 'grange' of Margam, this was never actually the case. The rules of the Cistercian Order regarding lay tenants were rescinded at this time, so there were no evictions of villagers such as had occurred at Sturmiestown and Llangewydd. Instead the inhabitants of the hamlet were allowed to remain, and it was run as a typical feudal manor with the Abbot as its lord. In no medieval document is it ever referred to as a grange. On the contrary, references to the pleas and perquisites issuing from its manorial court confirm that this was definitely not the case.

Echoes of Earl Gilbert's reorganisation of the former Lordship of Margam are to be found in the Inquisition Post Mortem made on the death of his son and successor, Richard, in 1262. This is the earliest surviving comprehensive record of the Lordship of Glamorgan. In it the manors of the Shire Fee are divided into two categories. By far the largest are those of the 'Old Feoffment' with a smaller section (which includes Newcastle[36] and Kenfig) showing manors of the 'New Feoffment'.

In England an identical division had been used to indicate manors in being at the death of King Henry I in 1135 as opposed to those created afterwards, particularly during the anarchy of the civil war. The same criteria cannot have applied to the Glamorgan manors which lay within a Marcher Lordship that was largely untouched by the sort of disruption that affected England. That this

---

[35] Documents relating to the earlier Sturmy manor indicate that in the north it stretched as far as the road along Cefn Cribwr ridge. The northern boundary of the later manor of Horgrove reached only part way up the south slope, and the land to the north of it can be subsequently shown to have been held by Welsh tenure. It is possible therefore that the Earl only removed the southern portion of Gryffydd Vychan's land that was already organised along feudal lines and allowed the family to retain the rest.

[36] It is sometimes stated that Newcastle passed to the Turbevilles of Coity on the marriage of Morgan Gam's daughter to Gilbert Turbeville. That this was not so is clearly illustrated by the fact that the manor was, for a time, in the hands of Earl Gilbert de Clare prior to the Turbervilles taking possession.

was so is indicated by the fact that the manor of Newton is included amongst the 'Old Feoffment' though we know that it was not created until after the year 1166. Penllyn, which was only 'granted out' by Earl William of Gloucester after 1147 is another case in point.

The division between the feoffments in Glamorgan's case therefore seems to date from the death of Earl William in 1183 which ushered in a period of anarchy similar to that in England 48 years earlier. Here the 'New Feoffment' therefore presumably listed the manors created either by Prince John or his successors Gilbert and Richard de Clare.

Morgan ap Caradoc, the Lord of Avan whose military operations had made the partial Welsh re-settlement of the coastal portion of Margam Lordship possible, died about the year 1208 and was succeeded by his sons Leison and Owain. These two are included with him on some of the charters

*Seal of Leision ap Morgan*

granted to the Abbey by their father towards the end of his life, and subsequently they issued several charters to the monks on their own behalf. Owain vanishes from the scene, about 1213-18 followed shortly after by Leison, and a new lord of Avan emerges in the shape of their younger brother Morgan Gam. Hitherto records of the period make no mention of him and Professor Beverly Smith (1958) suggests that this sequence of events perhaps indicates an internal power struggle for control of the Avan Lordship. Leision first managed to oust Owain, then Morgan in turn ousted Leision. Such an internal conflict within the house of Avan may be the reason why Earl Gilbert was able to secure the removal of the Welsh from both Newcastle and Kenfig without immediately provoking outright war

Unfortunately the documents upon which I base my reconstruction of 'what happened next' are undated, so the sequence of events I suggest may be a little awry, but Morgan certainly seems to have wasted no time in setting out his stall to regain the manor of Newcastle using force if necessary. The monks of Margam, all too aware of the coming storm, took the precaution of securing his seal to a charter (Birch, 1897: 230) promising not to "trouble them in their cultivated lands in the fee of Newcastle whilst Newcastle is not in his hands, not withstanding he may make war with others for the said Newcastle". They also took the further step of securing from the new Lord of Avan another document (Birch, 1897: 231) whereby he confirmed the grants made by Earl Gilbert in that manor which were actually those originally made by Welsh tenants under Morgan's father! It is quite a remarkable document in itself in that a minor magnate here confirms the chartered grants of his feudal overlord! Both documents seem therefore to relate to an early stage in this dispute when Morgan was keen to secure the Abbot's goodwill, whilst the latter was desperate to ensure that whatever the outcome the former Welsh properties would remain in monastic hands.

The Earl for his part cleverly used Newcastle to drive a wedge between Morgan Gam and Gilbert Turberville of Coity who, as Morgan's son-in-law was perhaps also his potential ally. He gave the manor and the castle to Gilbert with the implicit but unspoken warning that if he wished to keep it then he should remember which side his bread was buttered! All three parties – Morgan, Gilbert de Clare, and the Abbot of Margam – were clearly drawing their battle lines ready for impending conflict

At this point it must have appeared to the monks, and probably to the burgesses of Kenfig as well, that war was imminent, yet curiously Morgan hung back from direct confrontation with his overlord and instead directed his opening salvoes at the Abbot and his monks. They now reaped a heavy price for the former Welsh lands they had acquired so cheaply.

Historians have often admitted to being puzzled as why the Welsh were such generous patrons of Margam Abbey on the one hand, yet often inflicted damage upon its property. Generally they dismiss it with a shrug – the Welsh being Welsh again. Yet, as we have seen, the latter had good reasons for both their 'generosity' and their subsequent conflict with the Abbey. I am no Nationalist (far from it!), but down the years I have become increasingly irked by the perception that our ancestors were semi-barbaric thieves, oath-breakers, and sheep rustlers to whom the Norman invasion brought an element of civilisation. History is written by the victors, and as we have seen they needed no lessons in these aspects of medieval life from the conquered! One of the ironies of this early period of our history is that the one Anglo-Norman in whom the local Welsh chieftains apparently placed any trust was that most despised of Anglo-Norman monarchs – King John!

In taking on the Abbot and the community at Margam the new Lord of Avan was not being a mere bully-boy seeking to force helpless monks to do his bidding. We are talking here of a time when everyone wholeheartedly believed that through its good offices on earth the church was their one and only hope of safe passage into the heaven of the hereafter. It was a weapon that Bishops, Abbots and priests exploited to the full with the threat of excommunication. The sufferings of life on earth were as nothing compared to an eternity in hell! It is therefore a measure of the injustice felt by Morgan and his followers (who undoubtedly included the Gillemichels and the sons of Herbert) that they were prepared to risk such a fate by protesting in the only way they knew how.

The campaign against the Abbey started quietly enough. Suddenly the Abbot found himself the recipient of writs ordering his appearance before Morgan's court in Aberafan, presumably to answer for arrears of rent due on the lands given to the monks both by his family and his people. This Earl Gilbert countered by invoking a ruling previously made by King John that all such actions were only to be dealt with either by himself or his Chief Justice (Birch, 1897: 237). He then issued an order to his sheriff to see that it was enforced (Birch, 1897: 237-8). Although Morgan refused to concede this point until the 1230s (Birch, 1897: 230-1), he nevertheless cast about for other means of bringing pressure to bear on the Abbot.

His next ploy was rather more subtle and resulted in the Earl issuing yet another charter (Birch, 1897: 238) ordering the Abbot not to 'entertain' or feed those proceeding to the Shire Court or to perform military service at Cardiff, or "its Welsh neighbours who trouble it with too many visits". Clearly Morgan and his countrymen were turning the Abbey's tradition of offering hospitality to travellers and the poor back on itself in a valiant attempt to eat the monks out of house and home!

Bolstered by the support of the Earl, the Abbot stood firm, so legal and economic means having failed to achieve a result, the Lord of Avan turned to more direct methods. According to the *Annals of Margam* (Luard, 1864) two Abbey granges were destroyed in the year 1223 and more than a thousand of its sheep butchered. Operations against the granges and the monks' flocks that were the mainstay of the community's economy, continued again the following year resulting in the deaths of two Abbey servants and a shepherd boy. A Morgan ab Owain (who was probably Morgan's nephew) carried out a raid on Neath Abbey burning 'the house of the monks' (perhaps some of the living accommodation at the Abbey), killing four servants and over 400 sheep. He too then turned his attention upon Margam, and later admitted causing damage amounting to £154 to Abbey property. Not much in today's terms, but a return of the lands held by the monks made to the parent house at Clairvaux in 1336 (Birch, 1897: 304-) places the sum in context. At that time the Abbey was farming some 6,300 acres of land (About 4,200 acres modern measure) and the value placed upon them was just over £75 – half that of the damage caused by Owain!

As expected and feared, open warfare then broke out and during the course of the year 1226. St. Nicholas, Laleston and Newcastle were all attacked and burned.

In 1227 'the Welsh' destroyed the Abbey grange at Penhydd (near Bryn, Port Talbot) killing many of the sheep and oxen there. Then they did the same at Resolven where another Abbey servant was killed, and then carried off flocks of sheep from the Grange of Theodoric in Avan Marsh. This provoked a response not only from the Earl but King Henry III as well. Both issued charters taking the Abbey under their protection, though neither seems to have been able to provide it with much in the way of practical assistance.

The monks of Margam also had a grange at Llangeinor (near Bridgend), and to judge from documents of the period, here too the local inhabitants (particularly those that had been ejected from their homes to create the grange) were giving them a hard time. This grange stood within an area encompassed by the parishes of Llangeinor and Llandyfodwg that belonged to the De Londres family of Ogmore Castle. In a charter he granted the monks some time prior to 1228, Morgan's cousin, Morgan ap Cadwallon of Glynrhondda, took this grange under his protection, and implies that he had succeeded in appropriating this territory for himself. This is indicated by the fact he also granted the monks freedom of pasture throughout his lands (Birch, 1897: 233) as far south as his boundary with the lordship of Coity. Morgan's lordship of Glynrhondda did not share a common boundary with Coity, so he had evidently taken possession of the De Londres land.

Morgan ap Cadwallon then goes on to state that to the west his land bordered that of Morgan Gam without any mention of Earl Gilbert de Clare's land of Tir Iarll in the Llynfi Valley. Again the implication is that he and his cousin now enjoyed total control of all the hill territory to the north of Kenfig and Coity.

Kenfig, be it noted, had so far escaped all the violence. Could it be that Morgan was unwilling to break friendly and commercial relationships fostered during the thirty and more years the 'free Welshmen' had occupied land near the town? Castle and town still remained in the hands of the Earl and the burgesses, but for how much longer was anyone's guess!

Then, during the year 1228, things changed dramatically. Morgan ap Cadwallon was captured by his cousin Hywel ap Maredudd of Miskin who not only had him blinded, but castrated as well. In so doing he seems to have been acting on his own behalf either to settle some old score or to secure possession of Morgan's land. At the same time Earl Gilbert somehow captured Morgan Gam and hustled him off into captivity in England 'loaded with chains'. The violence in Glamorgan nevertheless continued with Hywel ap Maredudd burning both St Hillary and St Nicholas (for the second time) the following year.

Any relief the burgesses of Kenfig may have felt at the removal of their dangerous neighbour soon turned to incredulity when Earl Gilbert released Morgan Gam less than twelvemonths after his capture and restored him to his land of Avan! Why, nobody knows. Morgan had to find sureties and hostages for his future good behaviour but even so the decision to release him is surprising to say the very least! Perhaps his cousin Hywel of Miskin was proving just as much of a handful and Morgan, having made his own peace with the Earl, undertook to ensure that in future he also toed the line. But there may have been another motive.

This was a time when Llewelyn Fawr the Prince of Gwynedd was carrying all before him throughout Wales. Hubert de Burgh (briefly the husband of Earl Gilbert's late Aunt Isabel of Gloucester) was at this time the King's Justiciar in Wales and massively unpopular with the Marcher Lords. Later they and Llewelyn combined against Hubert to bring about his downfall in 1232, so perhaps De Clare was using Morgan to make some early overtures towards the Welsh Prince with a view to bringing about just such an alliance. The truth will, however, never be known for Earl Gilbert died in 1230. His heir Richard was only a boy of eight and King Henry III took control of his land on his behalf. For

Glamorgan this meant that the hated Hubert de Burgh was appointed to administer the Lordship for the King. So far as the Welsh Lords of Glamorgan were concerned, when that happened, any previous agreements concluded with the late Earl Gilbert were null and void and Morgan launched a major offensive aimed at both Neath and Kenfig.

In 1231 Prince Llewelyn invaded South Wales apparently in an attempt to give practical assistance to his supporters in Glamorgan and Gwent. He failed to take Caerleon castle (which he perhaps intended to recover on behalf of Morgan ap Hywel), but met with better fortune when he marched west and combined with Morgan Gam to overrun the castle and town of Neath. The *Annals of Margam* (Luard, 1864) tell us that the Welsh left Neath "without any inhabitants" which some have taken to mean that there was a wholesale massacre. Had that been the case then I'm pretty sure the monastic scribe would not have hesitated to say so, adding some gory details to illustrate the point as well. Rather it would seem that Morgan simply drove out the remnants of the garrison and the townsfolk then razed the buildings to the ground. Following this success, Llewelyn headed back off to North Wales, but as refugees from Neath trickled into their town the people of Kenfig can have been under no illusion that they were next on Morgan's list!

It had now been 46 years since the burgesses had actually needed to fight to protect their homes, and there can have been few amongst them who still remembered the events of 1183-5. Despite the uneasiness of the peace, the town had apparently flourished, for there is mention of buildings outside its walls and others built so close to the castle that they had to be removed so as not to hinder its defence against the impending attack. This implies an expansion of the original settlement within the town walls, and it would not surprise me to discover that the number of burgages it contained at this time exceeded the highest ever figure of 144 from available records.

Both garrison and townsfolk had probably been at a state of high alert ever since Earl Gilbert booted the Welsh out of Kenfig territory and Newcastle, and it is doubtful in fact whether they had ever completely relaxed their guard during the long years of peace. This was something that was borne in on me when I was reading the Ordinances of the Borough of Cowbridge.

These had probably been copied from those of Kenfig about 1249-54 but when the job was done the burgesses of the new town realised there was a serious omission, and made a very necessary amendment. This is in the form of a rider added to Ordinance No 20, which actually deals with the practice of unfair trading by Burgesses making private deals:

> Ytt is Ordained that every burgesse, tenante, reciante, and inhabitante of the said towne shall have a defencible weapon and harnes (armour) after his abilitie, to stand by the Baillifes, Aldermen and other officers of the said towne, for the defence and good order of the same.

At Kenfig the almost constant threat of danger ever since the town had been founded apparently rendered such a bylaw superfluous because the need for its inhabitants to have arms and armour was so obvious as to be self-evident.

So throughout the winter of 1231/2 the burgesses looked to their weapons and drilled and practised their combat skills under the watchful eyes of Portreeve and Constable. The latter was a man named William de Rievalle, and it was he who was probably in overall charge of the defence. He also had a secret weapon, for within the Welsh ranks there was a 'mole' keeping him abreast of developments within Morgan's household. As winter turned to spring and the Easter festival approached Rievalle was therefore made aware of the day and the date on which the impending attack would be launched.

This enabled him to make the final preparations for the defence. Some buildings inside the town were deliberately removed by controlled burning. Erected during the years of peace these had encroached rather too close to the castle walls for comfort, providing cover from which an enemy assault could be launched. The burgesses for their part removed some of their most valuable property – their dairy cattle – from the town, taking them to hiding places in the surrounding dunes and marshes.

Both measures seem to indicate that realistically the defenders did not expect to be able to hold the town wall against a determined assault which meant that the non-combatants – the women children and the elderly – were at risk. De Rievalle would not have wanted them inside the castle where their presence would only have hindered his garrison. Instead it was arranged that when the Welsh arrived they were to take refuge in the church and its graveyard in the hope that the Welsh would respect the sanctity of the site. Then there was nothing left to do but wait.

Morgan's army duly arrived to find the town gates locked against them. The burgesses would have been too few in number to man the entire perimeter of their defences, so the intention would have been to concentrate in numbers at whichever point the main attack developed. But Morgan also had a trick or two up his sleeve. The Margam scribe who has left us this description of the attack tells us that the Welsh opened the proceedings by setting fire to buildings that stood outside the town wall and ditch. The smoke from these would have provided excellent cover under which their assault could be launched. With the wind in the right direction flames and sparks from the burning buildings would also have blown towards the wooden palisade, and into the thatched buildings of the town beyond, creating secondary fires.

The heat and the smoke driven into the faces of the defenders made it difficult for them to see what was happening and where the attackers were gathering. All speculation and conjecture ended when, with a great shout, Morgan's army launched itself upon the town.

Over the town ditch they scrambled, up the bank on the opposite side, and over the palisade, into the town itself. The defence crumbled, and soon the defenders were streaming back towards the castle pursued by the Welsh. Once inside, the burgesses took their places alongside Rievalle's garrison as the pursuers poured through the town streets ransacking and burning their homes.

Several documents from this period indicate that the church and its graveyard immediately adjoined the castle with the cemetery wall bordering the defensive ditch of the castle's outer ward. The burgesses could only watch helplessly therefore as the Welsh swept into this area where their families had taken refuge. Morgan was nevertheless quickly on the scene and, having ascertained that the refugees here were indeed only women, children and the elderly, gave orders that they were not to be harmed. It was an action that amazed the Margam scribe, and is perhaps a reflection of how Welsh attitudes towards the town of Kenfig had been changed by their experience during the years of peace. Maybe Morgan even had it in mind to allow the town to continue if his assault upon the castle succeeded, as initially seemed likely when his men successfully drove the defenders from its outer walls.

De Rievalle, however, must have been a determined and able commander, for he rallied his men and somehow managed to stem the tide. The Welsh had not come equipped for a siege which would have been the next logical step, so taking what they could carry from the shops and houses in the town, they withdrew leaving the burgesses to salvage what they might from their ravaged homes and businesses.

Thanks to the unknown scribe at Margam we know more details about the 1232 attack upon Kenfig than any other. Morgan's failure to take the town and castle was decisive, and brought the war that had started back in 1167 to a rather surprisingly but abrupt conclusion. This was not the end of the Welsh attacks on Kenfig—far from it—but it was the end of the sustained pressure by the Lords of

Avan to secure total control of that part of Glamorgan west of the river Ogmore.

In the years that followed 1232 we see Morgan Gam acting in the role of peacemaker, presiding over a series of quit-claims by which his followers and allies surrendered their disputed lands to the Margam monks. Morgan and Bishop Elias of Llandaff also brought to an end the dispute between Rees Coch and the monks over Llangeinor grange in 1234 (Birch, 1897: 246) and this was followed by a whole raft of individual agreements involving other Welshmen who had been causing problems for the monks there. Similar quit-claims relating to disputed land in Avan Marsh were made during this period prior to 1240.

Closer to Kenfig, Morgan himself was present when Llewelyn Bren and Llewelyn Hen surrendered their claim to former Gillemichel land adjoining Waunbant Road, Kenfig Hill (Birch, 1897: 253) as did Ketherick and Ivor, the sons of William Gillemichel. Also, Ener ap Canaythur gave up his claim to part of a moor at Tre-y-Gedd near Baiden, and Morgan ab Owain agreed to pay the monks compensation for the damage he had caused to Abbey property. We have already noted that this amounted to £153 which, in the context of the time, was an enormous sum. It nevertheless pales into insignificance besides the damages of £324 claimed against the sons of Alaythur! They had apparently had a hand in the destruction of Penhydd grange in 1227, but did not finally concede the Abbot's claim against them until 1246. In 1234 the sons of Gryffydd Vychan and Alice Sturmy also admitted that their claim against the Abbey for the rent due upon the monastic half of the former Sturmy manor was false.

Morgan's successors at Avan showed no inclination to resurrect the family's claim to Newcastle and the former Lordship of Margam, so after his death in 1240 the monks were able to continue securing their hold on the land they had acquired. In truth, they emerged as the greatest beneficiaries of the conflict in which they had acquired great swathes of territory between the rivers Kenfig and Ogmore. They were to retain all of theses until the Abbey itself was no more.

The war between the House of Avan and the Lords of Glamorgan therefore ended with both sides virtually back where they started in 1167. Nevertheless the area in and about Kenfig had been altered in a manner that affected the course of its history for many centuries, even after the town, the castle and the Abbey had long ceased to exist. When Margam Abbey was dissolved by Henry VIII almost all its land between the rivers Ogmore and Avan was acquired by the Mansels of Penrice making them by far the largest single landowner in the district with the capacity to affect local affairs for good or ill.

# Chapter 8

## OUR TOWN AND BOROUGH

Although it would not have been apparent to the burgesses of Kenfig at the time, the repulse of Morgan Gam's army in 1232 had won them the right to exist. Attacks by the Welsh and others upon their town were to continue for almost another century, but these were just raids – demonstrations of protest or means of gaining plunder. What though of the town itself? Only fragments of the castle are still visible today, but over the past dozen years I have been able to recover some details of the physical appearance of Kenfig from various documents that have survived from the medieval period.

**The Borough Boundary.**
The burgesses usually referred to their community as "Our Town and Borough", a phrase that perhaps needs a little explanation. Today we tend to consider these as separate elements—the walled town and the area of land within which it stood where burgess' rights applied. I have used this modern application in these notes, but it is not the way the medieval burgesses saw their situation. To them the town was the borough, and the borough was the town— the two words were virtually interchangeable.

Rights conferred by charter upon the inhabitants of Kenfig applied throughout the area of the borough. All who lived within its borders were free men and not subject to the whims of any manorial lord but were governed by a Portreeve, his council, and the town Ordinances. But what were those boundaries? They are set out in a charter granted to the town by Thomas le Despenser in 1397 (Gray, 1909) and were those his father Edward had confirmed by another charter issued in 1360. He in turn would have taken these from an even earlier charter that is now lost, and so on back to the very first earlier one issued by Earl Robert of Gloucester prior to his death in 1147. Thomas added certain additional rights, but the boundaries themselves had probably remained more or less constant throughout the entire period.

Although the charter gives the boundaries in some detail, the description is confusing and seems to have rather befuddled past historians. It was the simple realisation that they are not in fact the boundaries of the borough that was abolished in 1886 that made it possible for me to locate all the various boundary marks showing that in fact the medieval Borough of Kenfig was considerably smaller than the one depicted on Victorian maps, This discovery has in turn given valuable clues to Kenfig's past, not least to the story of its eventual downfall as will be related in the next chapter. Here, however, we are merely interested in the boundaries themselves.

Some of the confusion in interpreting the description from the 1360 charter is that it does not follow the normal practice of describing the boundaries in the form of a circuit. Instead the writer gives those on the east; then the west, followed by north and south respectively. Once that is realised it is then possible with the aid of a little local knowledge to reconstruct a perambulation of the entire circuit in a clockwise direction starting at a location called 'Howlotesford' — 'The Owlet's Ford'.

This lay on the River Kenfig and is almost certainly the location of the existing ford and footbridge adjoining Llanmihangel Farm. Some years ago the farmer discovered a large stone lying in the ford that displayed clear (if well worn) evidence of some sort of design cut into one side. (It is now displayed in the garden wall of the farm.) It was identified as being the head of a Celtic cross dating from the pre-Norman period which has led to speculation that a chapel may have existed in the immediate vicinity. Such crosses were, however, often erected in open country and, given the location of the find, I believe that it had probably been re-used by the burgesses to mark the point on the ford where their boundary struck inland from the river towards Mawdlam.

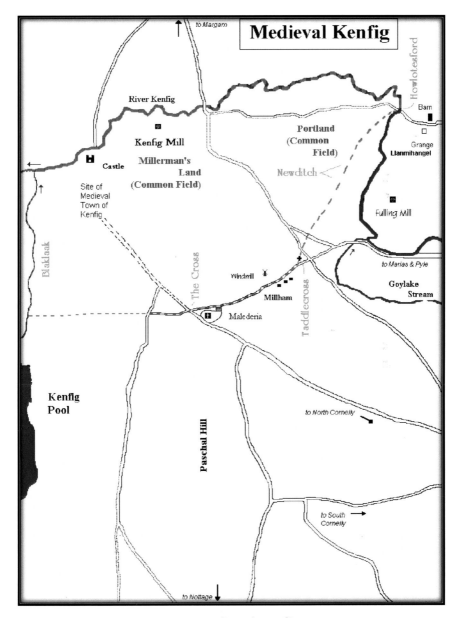

*Map 4: Medieval Kenfig*

**The Road to Margam crossing Mont Mawr (Millhill).**
In the early 17th century the land on the far side of the road was known as *Tir Ffin* (Land's End), a memory of the time when it had been the part of the borough furthest from the town.

*Llanmihangel Mill Farm (Howlotesford?)*

Three centuries later their successors similarly re-utilised part of a pre-Norman Christian monument to mark their boundary on Water Street, Margam. From the ford, the boundary headed away south-east from the river to 'Newditch'. This is referred to as "the new foss" in a Margam charter of 1266 (Birch, 1897: 285) which makes it clear that it was associated with an enclosure called Portland. This is still there today: a large enclosure encompassing land above the river on the Kenfig side of the ford. The name indicates that it belonged to the burgesses of Kenfig (the word 'port' then meant 'a trading-place' rather than a harbour) and was probably one of their common fields divided into plots of land about an acre or so in extent.

After the 'New Ditch' the boundary (which may have at this point been physically marked by a bank and ditch) also separated "the land of the Abbey of Margam and the land of the Abbey of Teokesburie" (Tewkesbury) as far as "Taddulcrosse".

The Sutton stone base of this cross, now known as 'Croes y Ddadl', is still there today. It lies in the north-west quadrant of land at the point where the road from North Cornelly to Margam is crossed by the land from Pyle to Mawdlam and is commonly known locally as Mawdlam Cross. The monument has a hole in the top which was the housing for the actual cross that was probably made of wood, and when erected it probably adjoined the original crossroads which have since 'moved' south in the face of sand-encroachment. How long the name 'Croes y Ddadl' (The Cross of Dispute) has been in existence I do not know. I suspect it is of fairly recent origin based upon an antiquarian interpretation that the earliest recorded name - 'Tadulcrosse' - was an English version of the pre-existing Welsh name. This may be right, but my own research has led me to another possibility which indicates that the name is of English origin. In Old English a 'tada' was a toad or frog, and each Spring this area is alive with thousands of toads making their way to their ancient spawning grounds in the wetlands around Kenfig Pool.

The boundary from Taddulcrosse was formed by "the highway leading from Taddulcrosse to the cross". Today this road is still there though sand-encroachment has probably moved it to a more southerly course than the original. I would guess that the next point on the circuit - 'the cross' - was the point where this road crossed the main highway from Kenfig to Cardiff (Heol Las) near Mawdlam church. From there it continued on to a T-junction with the old road from Kenfig town to Nottage, now marked by a sharp, right-angled bend on the road to modern-day Kenfig. The continuation of the former Nottage road towards the medieval town can still be traced for a short distance beyond this corner until it vanishes beneath the sand.

*A simple plank bridge carries a footpath across a muddy hollow that is perhaps the former bed of the Blaklaak or one of its tributaries*

From 'the cross' the boundary continued a short distance towards the coast as far as a stream called 'The Blaklaak'. This had already vanished beneath the sand in 1360 but, as the text of the charter explains, it "used to run from the southern water to the northern water of Kenfeg". In fact it is thought to have been the overflow of Kenfig Pool, diverted northwards to the river when drainage directly towards the sea became blocked by the coastal dunes.The Blaklaak then formed the western limit of the borough to the point where it drained into the Kenfig, and the boundary then continued up the centre of the river to Howlotesford which was our starting point. From this it is clear that it was considerably smaller than the later borough. It did not extend northwards beyond the river towards Margam nor west as far as the sea, and Mawdlam church lay outside its boundary.

## The Common and Fields
These were the limits of the franchise of Kenfig Borough within which land not occupied by town or castle was utilised either as arable or common pasture. Occasional gifts of property by burgesses to Margam Abbey indicate that their arable land was contained within large enclosures like Portland lying on the higher ground to the east and south of the borough. A common field called 'Mullermanisland' ('Miller man's Land') lay between the castle and the present road from Cornelly to Margam. Other arable plots seem to have been located around the summit of Mont Mawr on the north side of the road from Taddulcrosse to 'the cross' though whether these were also contained within a larger enclosure is not known.

The Kenfig Society excavations immediately west of the castle bailey uncovered traces of medieval ploughing etched into the boulder clay underlying the sand at this point. These have proved impossible to date, but may represent attempts by the earliest settlers to raise crops here when the infant town was still contained within the castle. We know that Robert Earl of Gloucester gave the monks of Ewenny Priory a burgage on the Blaklaak stream outside the western gate of this early town which must be somewhere in the vicinity of the area under investigation. He also gave them 21 acres of arable land adjoining Kenfig River, and although the full details of the location are not given, it may be that it was their tenants who ploughed the land here.

What seems certain is that any attempt to produce corn on this land was not very successful. When excavated, the furrows in the clay were filled with sand, leading us to believe that the original layer of topsoil was quite thin, and was eventually quite literally blown away by the wind. Once the burgesses had settled into their new home they probably abandoned all attempts to farm in this area in favour of better and deeper soils elsewhere.

As water cannot penetrate the clay sub-soil on the lowlands around and about the town, the land in its immediate vicinity must have been rather wet and marshy. What was not enclosed for arable

*The Dune System west of Mawdlam extending to the coast.*
*The nearest copse of trees on the right of this picture*
*is largely composed of alder trees which only normally occur*
*on the banks of streams and rivers.*

purposes therefore became the town common upon which the burgesses (and only the burgesses) could pasture livestock. In the main these seem to have been dairy cattle – each burgess keeping one or two cows and turning the milk into butter and cheese to feed their household. Corn for bread they grew on their plots at Portland, Millermansland, and elsewhere. Following standard medieval practice one of these fields would have been allowed to lie fallow every year for the soil to recover and during this time their cattle would have been turned into it to graze and further improve the soil with manure.

Although not mentioned, horses belonging to the burgesses would also have been put on the common to graze, and possibly pigs, though it would seem from the Ordinances (Gray, 1909) that the latter were normally kept in the town where they made a useful contribution by disposing of any edible refuse! Ordinance No. 23 imposed a five shilling fine upon any burgess who erected a pigsty to the annoyance of his neighbour "unless and except it be in his garden within the walls of the said town". An official known as The Keeper of the Cross was to have fourpence out of the shilling fine due on every pig he caught straying in the area of the market cross. A rider to the bye-law (No. 28) required that those owners who turned their swine onto the common insert a ring in the nose of each animal to prevent them rooting up the vegetation. This, however, I believe may be a later addition to the Ordinances perhaps made when the sand incursion onto the common had begun to cause alarm, or even perhaps later when the town itself had ceased to exist.

## The Town

In attempting to reconstruct some idea of the layout of the town of Kenfig I have, of course, to rely almost totally on information contained in documents of the period, as not a trace of it is visible today. We know that it was surrounded by a ditch and a wall – the latter probably of timber rather than masonry – in which were set a number of gates that were guarded day and night. During the day the gatekeepers kept a wary eye on those entering and leaving. At dusk the gates were closed, and remained so throughout the hours of darkness.

It also seems safe to assume that, in common with other contemporary Welsh Borough towns, the streets inside the walls were laid out in a grid-iron pattern. The principal street was the High Street, and bearing in mind that Kenfig lay on the main highway through South Wales, it would have most likely been part of this 'through route'. The location of the castle between the town and the river means that the road from Margam can only have entered around one end of its fortifications. The eastern side seems the more likely as the town gate and the adjoining ford or bridge across the river would here have been commanded by the castle keep. From this north gate the road would have passed through the town in more or less a straight line to another gate on the south from whence it continued across the common to Mawdlam church.

The importance of High Street to the town is reflected in the Ordinances, and as a 'through road' for travellers it was important that it should not be obstructed in any way. Butchers were not to use it to "slay any manner of victuall, neither make any scalding", nor deposit there "heads, feet, nor none other garbage". Their trade was, according to another bylaw, only to be carried on in The Shambles — a street or area of the town specifically set aside for their use.

The High Street is also mentioned in other bye-laws aimed at preventing obstructions on the town streets by such activities as playing football and tennis, milking cows, or penning cattle there. Despite its grand title, however, it would have appeared very narrow to our eyes. Locally this is well illustrated by Elder Street at Bridgend which was formerly the main street of that town. It would also have been none too clean! The sewerage system was usually a gutter running down the centre of the road and emptying into the river. A convenient stream was sometimes diverted into these gutters to flush everything away, but this was not normally the case.

Other than liquid deposited by the householders it required a good downpour of rain to flush everything away properly.

There was no municipal refuse service with responsibility for keeping the streets clean "from dung and other filth", and likewise no municipal body to ensure that they were paved or cobbled. That task was allocated to the householders themselves – "every man to pave the same ... before his door". Similarly everyone was responsible for disposing of their own refuse in a responsible manner. Most households had a kitchen midden or refuse heap somewhere on the premises where garbage was allowed to mount up until eventually carted away. Some used it to manure their plots of land in the fields, others merely deposited it upon the common. It was with this in mind that another Ordinance made it an offence to dump "dust, dung, nor noe other filth in the streets, nor in the town ditches, nor within fifty foot of any of the gates of the said town, or any part of the walls".

High Street probably connected with the market place – an open area that was at the very heart of the community physically and commercially. It was marked by a cross, and was the preserve of the official known as 'The Keeper of the Cross'. We know of him only from the Ordinance which gave him the right to impound any pigs he found straying there. I would presume however that this was not his only function in life and, given the location, he may also have been responsible for supervising the placing of stalls during the weekly markets and annual fairs, collecting the fees, and other such duties.

The prime location for those seeking to sell their wares in the market was in the arcade beneath the Town Hall. As this is often referred to as 'The Guildhall' it would appear that its construction and maintenance was a joint venture by the town council and the Guild of Cordwainers and Glovers. It adjoined the market-place itself, and references to it in the Ordinances indicate that it followed the standard pattern of such halls elsewhere in that it was raised upon pillars with the market in the sheltered area beneath. Access to the hall was by an external stairway at one end beneath which was the town lock-up or gaol. This is also mentioned in the bye-laws as burgesses could opt to be imprisoned instead within the main hall provided that they were able and willing to find suitable sureties against their escape.

Of the other streets in the town we know the names of four, High Street and The Shambles where the butchers plied their trade have already been mentioned. East Street presumably ran from a gate on the east side of town and is presumed to have continued westwards through the town (as 'West Street'?) to another on that side. It would therefore have bisected High Street, probably in the immediate vicinity. of the market place. The gate on the town's East-gate gave access to the town mill and the common Fields at Mullermansland and Portland. If (as seems likely) there was another gate on the west, then this would have opened into the area between the town and the Blaklaak Stream where excavations by the Kenfig Society seem to indicate the existence of an industrial area in the 13th century.

Monk or Monekin Street was where Margam Abbey had created a grange out of burgages given them by pious inhabitants the possession of which then allowed them to trade within the town as 'out-burgesses'. From the information about it contained within their charters, this street seems to have extended southwards from East Street (or its western continuation) and lay west of, and roughly parallel to, High Street.

The houses that lined these and any other streets at Kenfig were the 'burgages' that are mentioned in the charters, each standing on its own 'burgage plot'. They varied in size from town to town, and short of excavation we have no indication of how large those at Kenfig were. What we can say is that they were almost certainly strips of land with the narrow sides aligned upon the street itself. Owning such a plot was the basic requirement for becoming a burgess. Some belonged to burgesses from elsewhere who utilised them as branches of their main business, though possession of such a plot did not allow them full burgess rights. These were confined to those who actually lived in the town.

Many, perhaps most of these burgages contained business premises built with a shop immediately fronting the road. Behind and above this were the living quarters of the occupier, his family, their servants and workers. At the rear of the buildings were the workshops, cattle stalls, stables, pig sties, garden, and in some cases a well. In the main, timber and clay were the materials used in their construction. The Kenfig Society's excavation (Robbins, 2002) (which is at a site which lay outside the town walls) uncovered the remains of a house or barn which may or may not be typical of the type of construction generally employed within the town and is in fact the earliest example of a 'clum' or 'clon' building (a term used to describe buildings made of clay) so far discovered in Wales.

Clay on its own is an excellent building material provided that water does not penetrate the bottom or the top of the walls. The builders therefore initially laid down a base made of stones with clay (rather than mortar) used as a bonding agent. The clay wall was then erected upon this, and was usually built up around hurdles so as to give it added strength. A section cut through the wall of the excavated building at Kenfig showed that this was not the case: there was no trace of any hurdles or internal support-timbers. Inside each corner of the building was a large stone set into the floor to provide a solid base for the timber uprights that supported the roof which would probably have been covered with thatch.

It is this combination of thatch and timber that made the town of Kenfig so vulnerable to fire whether started deliberately by attackers or accidentally. In 1228, for example, it is recorded that many burgages were destroyed in a fire started by a lightning strike on one of its houses. Our excavations indicate that about the middle of that century a blacksmith was working in this area outside the walls, and I have often wondered if he was forced to move his business here outside the walls because of the danger of fire from his forge. At the same time the Borough Ordinances place no restrictions on the siting of such businesses, nor on those of the 'oven keepers' who baked bread for the town bakers and households alike.

### The Church of Saint James.
Besides the castle and the guildhall the other substantial and important building within the walls was the church dedicated to Saint James. Documents also mention a chapel of Saint Thomas, but this I believe was probably the garrison chapel and situated within the castle's fortifications. As seems to have been the case in most medieval towns the church was probably set back

*The font at Mawdlam church believed to have originally come from that of Saint James at Kenfig.*

from the market place that was the town's commercial heart around which would have been some of the most sought-after burgage plots in the community. The church stood within a burial ground that on its northern side bordered the defences of the castle's outer ward.

Discoveries of human remains in an area about 300 yards south of the castle keep during the late 19th and early 20th century seem to confirm such a location, and records tell us that the graveyard was planted with trees and shrubberies. Used as we are to cemeteries full of gravestones this may seem a little odd, but is an indication of how our perception of graveyards has altered over the centuries. In the main the memorials in even our oldest graveyards only date from the end of the 18th century — anything older is usually found inside the church itself. Although our ancestors buried the remains of their loved ones with no less reverence than we do today, to them the graveyard was a recreational area. Here were held 'church ales' — parties at which ale, brewed by the church wardens to raise money for the upkeep of the building, was freely available. The walls of the church were used by the local youth for playing ball games. As late as 1787 it is recorded that the windows of Pyle church were covered by shutters in order to facilitate this practice. At Mawdlam a game involving the throwing of a ball over the church tower was traditionally played at the festival of Saint Mary Magdalene well into the 19th century.

Of the appearance of the building itself we have no record, but we do have one or two small clues. Because its stones were reused to build a new parish church of Saint James at Pyle in the 15th century we know that it was a substantial building made from carefully shaped blocks of stone. I am doubtful, however, as to whether the church at Kenfig would have had a tower at one end as was the case with its successor. Given the town's violent history and the church's proximity to the castle, it may be that such a development would have been considered undesirable.

## The People

By and large the people of medieval Kenfig are but barely apparent in the pages of history. We know the names of some from documents of the period, and a few of these achieved a slight prominence by donations of land and houses to the monks at Margam Abbey. Sometimes there is a mention of their occupation, but really we know virtually nothing about them other than their names.

What we can say is that their lives revolved about the need to defend their homes and to secure a living sufficient to feed themselves, their wives and their family. Although most, perhaps every household, aimed at a certain degree of self-sufficiency through growing crops and keeping livestock, it was the trade of the town which almost everyone relied on, from the wealthiest merchant to the pot-boy at a local tavern.

This fact is trumpeted throughout the town Ordinances. Naturally there are laws dealing with local government and others aimed at ensuring an acceptable standard of behaviour amongst its citizens, but the bulk of them are concerned with setting standards for trader and craftsmen alike.

'Forestalling' was a problem that commonly affected market towns. The principal was that any goods brought into the town for sale were not to be sold before they had been offered in the market place. There were certain limited exceptions, but fair trading practice dictated that in general everyone should be entitled to have a chance to buy. The number of Ordinances relating to this is perhaps an eloquent testimony to the fact that the principle was not infrequently breached by some of the community's more unscrupulous dealers!

The standards of goods and services offered in the town were also regulated by the Ordinances with the exception of those of the cordwainers and glovers who had their own craft guild. These by-laws give us an indication of some of the trades carried on in Kenfig as well as the problems associated with them. We have already noted some of the problems with the butchers who not only provided meat for the table but the raw materials for the leather trade, and also noted the regulation relating to the tanners in connection with their branch of the industry. Most important of all, however, was the work of the bakers and their associates the oven-keepers.

Bread was the staple food of a medieval community, so it is not surprising that the very first Ordinance on the roll deals with the work of the bakers. In order to practice in the town they needed a licence from the Portreeve, and were required to "bake good and sufficient bread …keeping such true size as shall be limited unto them by the Portreeve, weighing according to the rate of the corn sold in the markett". Furthermore their produce was to be freely available to all – "burgesses, chencers, inhabitants and strangers". Failure to meet these standards rendered them liable to a heavy fine determined by the Portreeve in addition to any penalties due under statute law (During the medieval period these would have been Marcher laws current within Glamorgan lordship.).

The kind of dodges bakers tended to employ to fleece their customers were many and varied. One of the commonest was to adulterate wheat flour with rye or beans. In another instance the additive was iron filings which helped produce a loaf of standard weight but not substance!

It seems that the actual baking of the loaves was often carried out by tradesmen called oven-keepers as a separate part of the baking process. Domestically as well as commercially obtaining a constant supply of timber to heat bread ovens must have been a considerable problem involving gathering and transporting large quantities of firewood. As well as the bakers therefore, many of the inhabitants who baked their own bread made use of the service offered by the oven-keepers. According to the Ordinances one of their favourite ploys was to take a little dough from each loaf brought to them to be baked and use this to make up new loaves which they then sold!

If bread was the staple food, then ale was the staple drink. Until the advent of proper water treatment and piped distribution in the 19th century, being a teetotaller was never really an option! Water sources (particularly in urban areas) were often heavily polluted. Our ancestors never appreciated that boiling water to make a mash during the brewing process removed most of these impurities, but experience taught them that ale was a healthier drink than water.

Healthiest of all was the 'third' or 'small' drink, so called because it was the last of three brews obtained from the same batch of mash. The first was the strongest, and the third fairly weak so it was this that was generally used simply to quench the thirst.

This trade was carried on by inn and alehouse keepers who brewed ale on their premises. The latter were divided into taverners (male) and tapsters (female) and the ale they produced could either be consumed on their premises or taken away in jugs for consumption at home. The tapsters are particularly singled out in the bye-laws over and above the general requirement on brewers to "brew good and wholesome ale, third drink and small drink". If one of them had more than three 'pottles' in her house, then she was not to refuse to sell her ale to any burgess, chencer or inhabitant of the town.

Many of Kenfig's people would have brewed their own ale and baked their own bread, so there was an ever-present danger that the activities of the commercial producers would corner the market in the grain required for the manufacture of both. To guard against this they were forbidden to purchase supplies at the Friday markets until after 12 midday in the summer and 11 am in the winter thereby allowing householders to satisfy their own needs first. According to the Ordinances other produce commonly on sale in the market place included fish, eggs, butter, cheese, capons, rabbits and chickens.

The burgesses of Kenfig also did what they could to ensure that the traveller visiting Kenfig was made welcome. Innkeepers and those alehouse keepers offering accommodation were required to advertise the fact with 'a sign at his door'. Traditionally this was by a bush suspended from a hook, and they were forbidden to turn away those seeking shelter on pain of a fine of twelve pence for each default. Other regulations relate to the manner in which the town's alehouses were run. No taverner was to conduct his premises in such a manner that it caused annoyance to his neighbours after ten o'clock at night, and rather surprisingly there was a complete embargo on playing games such as dice, cards and bowls on premises of any description within the town. Similarly "licentious naughtipacks, bawdrey, or suspected harlotts, vagabonds, nor loyterers" were not to be harboured on licensed premises or elsewhere. Whilst 'Houses of ill-Repute' were therefore officially unwelcome at Kenfig, human nature being what it is I suspect this Regulation was another honoured more in the breach than the observance!

A licence was required from the Portreeve and council to carry on many of the businesses mentioned in the Ordinances, but stray documentary finds and references indicate that other legal but unregulated businesses also existed here. Blacksmiths are frequently mentioned. Traditionally they shod the horses that were the transport of the age, but in medieval times and afterwards this formed but a small element of their trade. They made the implements the burgesses required to work their land or for manufacture; they produced the nails and hinges needed to build their homes and the weapons and armour with which to defend them. Evidence from the site being excavated outside the town by the Kenfig Society also indicates that during the latter part of the 13th century iron was being smelted and worked there, probably using ore gathered in the vicinity.

The mention of a fuller suggests that there was at some time a small woollen industry in the town which, together with the shoemakers and glovers provided the stock in trade of the 'clothiers' who also appear in contemporary documents. Perhaps the most unusual occupation was that of 'Ernulf the Map Maker' who occurs in documents of the late 12th century. To these we must add carpenters, masons and thatchers and the like who, whilst they find no reference in the records, would inevitably have been found at a town like Kenfig at this period.

Finally there is the possibility that there was a potter working in the community at some time. Our excavation team had been alerted to this fact by the stray find, many years ago, of a small flattish pebble now in the possession of Mr John Blundell of Nottage. This had previously been picked up by his father in the area where their excavation was taking place, and was of interest in that a conical hole was partially bored into one side. The best explanation for this was that it had formed a bearing for the spindle of a potter's wheel. When therefore towards the end of one season they began finding scraps of unfired pottery associated with a burnt area of ground in one area of exploration it did not come as a complete surprise. Unfortunately they were unable to continue exploring at this location the following year because of an outbreak of foot and mouth disease across Britain, and other reasons have since intervened to prevent them continuing up to the time of writing. As a consequence it has therefore proved impossible to date this period of industrial activity.

The same site also yielded numerous fragments of broken pots dumped here as part of the town's rubbish. In the main these are imported ware brought to Kenfig from Bristol having been purchased by merchants from the town and sold across the counters of their shops to customers. The latter were drawn not just from the ranks of the inhabitants but beyond, for prior to the creation of the borough towns at Cowbridge and Aberafan in the middle of the 13th century, Kenfig was the only one between Neath in the west and Cardiff in the east.

Highlight of the commercial year at Kenfig were the two fairs held annually under the provisions of its charters. The principal one started on the eve of the festival of Saint James the Apostle (24th July) who was the town's patron saint, and lasted for eight days. A shorter three-day fair started on the Monday of Whitsun week. When a fair was in progress at any of the chartered towns in Glamorgan lordship the traders at the remainder were required to shut down their businesses for the duration. Presumably therefore when the Kenfig Fairs were held many of those from elsewhere set up stalls in the market-place here. Saint James's Fair would therefore have been a major local event with the town crammed with the booths and stalls of merchants offering goods and produce not normally available locally. With street entertainers, hucksters, pick-pockets and the rest, it would have been a raucous, vibrant and lively scene that was lost forever when the townsfolk eventually packed their bags and abandoned their town to the sand.

## The Kenfig Mills[37]

Beyond the walls of the town but still within the Borough were two corn mills. The first was a water mill built by Earl William of Gloucester in the early days of the town's existence. It lay between the castle and Pont Felin Newydd, and probably at a location just east of the present M4 viaduct where some ruins were uncovered during the laying of a pipeline in the 1990s. Because of the depth of the sand at this point and the gravel ballast of the adjoining railway marshalling yard, the sides of the trench were too unstable to permit a proper investigation, and no artefacts were apparent that might assist in dating the features. What was revealed was merely part of a wall (in which clay had been used to bond the stones) and a small section of stone-flagged floor. Nevertheless the features were at a location where, in theory, Kenfig's water mill would have been.

The mill drew its water from the river via a leat that began on the far side of Pont Felin Newydd (The name New Mill Bridge refers to a later mill built in the early 17th century on the opposite bank of the river at this point.) and was noted by local historian Thomas Gray (1909) passing beneath the original bridge in a culvert when the structure was demolished at the end of the 19th century. Although we know that a bridge existed here in the middle of the 13th century, the arrangement seems to indicate that the road it carries (linking North Cornelly and Margam) was not here at the time Kenfig was founded. Had this been the case then the leat would most likely have been started a little further downstream. When the road arrived the leat was already in existence and provision had to be made for it when the bridge was constructed. From this it follows that this road probably developed as a shortcut used by travellers by-passing the Borough on their way along the South Wales coast.

---

[37] For a more detailed history of these mills, and how their locations were identified, see my booklet *The Five Mills of Kenfig* published by The Kenfig Society in 2002.

Being outside the town walls this mill must have been an easy target for the Welsh in their attacks upon Kenfig, and there are indeed several references to its destruction during local uprisings.

The watermill was owned by Kenfig's lord who was almost invariably the Lord of Glamorgan. A second, slightly later mill though, was a piece of private enterprise on the part of one of the town's burgesses. It was a windmill that stood on the ridge we now call Mont Mawr, though the older name was 'Windmill Hill' or simply 'Mill Hill'. Documents of the period show that in the 13th century much of this ridge was occupied by plots of arable land owned by burgesses, probably lying within a large enclosure such as the ones at Millermansland and Portland.

Windmills began to be introduced into Britain in the late 12th century though the earliest indications that one stood on Mont Mawr only appear in documents from 1336 onwards. References to 'Millmotte' shows that it was raised on an artificial mound, and it was undoubtedly a 'post mill'. This meant that the mill itself was built on a large upright post about which it could be rotated to face into the direction from which the wind was blowing. If this sounds a rather precarious style of construction, that is nothing less than the truth! The whole thing was so top-heavy that a sudden change in direction by a strong wind or gale could topple it over. The miller therefore had to be on the alert for such changes twenty-four hours a day, ready to turn his mill at every shift of the wind!

A small hamlet grew up adjoining the mill on the road from Mawdlam to Pyle. Called Millhamme in 14th century documents it was later known as Millhill, and continued in existence up to the end of the 17th century. In later documents the houses mentioned here all lay on the south side of this road: which, since it was the boundary of the medieval borough, meant they actually stood just outside its borders. The mound upon which this mill stood may in fact have been the early castle that is mentioned in documents dating from the middle of the 13th century (see Appendix I for details about this).

Although not really part of Kenfig's story, I should in passing make some mention of two other mills that stood on Kenfig River but on the opposite bank. The property of Margam Abbey they are first mentioned in 1291 though they had probably been in existence for some considerable time prior to this. The one was Llanmihangel Mill which ground corn, and the other (a little further downstream) was probably a fulling mill processing woollen cloth. Primarily they were used just for supplying the needs of the Abbey community, but it would not be unusual to find that the monks were happy to earn some added income for their community by processing grain and wool from the lay community.

*Mawdlam: The main road into Kenfig from Cardiff*
*When the medieval town was in existence the road descended the ridge to the site of the town in the vicinity of the castle, the ruins of which lie in the middle distance*

## The 'Malederia'

In the year 1202 a Richard de Dunster gave Margam Abbey his burgage in the town of Kenfig, and an acre of land "outside the town near the Malederia" (Birch, 1897: 65). A malederia was a hospital or leper house, and such scanty evidence offered but little hope of ever identifying its actual location. By good fortune however some other clues have come to light over the years, and it now seem that it was probably located at the chapel of Saint Mary Magdalene. The reasons for believing this to be the case are more fully set out in Appendix VII.

This chapel stood just outside the boundaries of the medieval borough and town, and on the main road leading there from Cardiff (Heol Las). An excavation carried out by Channel Four's *'Time Team'* on a leper house just outside the town limits of Winchester revealed the layout of the complex of buildings there which were likewise associated with a chapel dedicated to Saint Mary Magdalene, and so it seems was very similar in form to ours.

At Winchester the chapel, the accommodation for the lepers, a cemetery and a house for the master in charge were all contained within an enclosure wall. At Mawdlam it seems that the leper accommodation was the building that is now The Angel Inn. Although much altered in the 1950s, photographs from the early part of the 20th century show a number of blocked-up doorways on the south (churchyard) side. Prior to alterations in the 1950s the main entrance was formerly situated on the other side. These indicate that like the leper house at Winchester the original building had been divided into five units – each providing accommodation for a leper and possibly their family. Today the inn lies outside the wall of the churchyard, but the alignment of this seems to indicate that originally it could have been contained within the walls. Certainly the fact that its main entrance and the blocked doorways originally faced the church seems to indicate that the two were formerly associated.

Locally it is claimed that The Angel was formerly an inn for pilgrims making their way to St David's cathedral, and in a strange way this may indeed be the case. Leprosy was a terrible disease that was greatly dreaded by medieval folk, and was believed to be a punishment inflicted by God for some sin or other committed by the sufferer. The one hope of a cure therefore was to secure God's forgiveness, which is why a chapel was normally associated with their accommodation. Two pilgrimages to the shrine of Saint David were considered the equivalent of one to Jerusalem itself, so by making such a long and arduous journey lepers hoped to secure divine forgiveness for their sins and thereby effect a cure.

So feared was leprosy by the people of the day that the unfortunate sufferers had to ring a hand-bell to give warning of their approach so people could avoid all contact with them. The malederia outside Kenfig therefore offered lepers alternative accommodation from that in the town or at Margam Abbey, and it was perhaps built by the burgesses and the monks for this purpose.

**The Government of the Town.**
The government of borough towns rested in the hands of the burgesses and was consequently something unique in the medieval period when normally those in whom authority was vested owed their position to an accident of birth. A runaway serf who successfully managed to live in the borough for a year and a day without being reclaimed by his lord became a free man, and in theory there was nothing to prevent him going on to become the governor of the community. To do so, however, he would first need to become a burgess which involved purchasing one of the burgages. He then presented himself before the town's Portreeve and Council to take the burgesses' oath.

It was the Portreeve who ruled Kenfig, and he was answerable only to the Constable of the Castle as the Lord's representative. Portreeves were elected annually, the burgesses submitting three names to the Constable who then made the final selection. During that year his word would be law within the borough boundaries. This position was reinforced by the provisions of the town Ordinances which were designed to give the holder of the office a status equal to that of the local gentry. He was the town magistrate before whom offenders against the Ordinances appeared and were punished, and it was he who, with the advice of his council, made the laws and rulings that governed the community. If he and the constable agreed that a particular law current in Glamorgan acted to the detriment of the town, then it could be declared null and void within its boundaries.

Inhabitants who believed they had a legal claim against the council were required to lay it before the Portreeve and not take it to one of the Lord's own courts. Such washing of the town's dirty linen in front of outsiders attracted one of the severest punishments in the Ordinance roll. In such cases the evidence was heard by a jury of six made up of three councillors and three 'commoners', i.e. those burgesses who were not on the council. Found guilty meant being 'discommoned' (disenfranchised) "for ever more" without any right of appeal, and a "grievous amerciament (fine) at the pleasure of the portreeve".

Other Ordinances made it an offence to utter "unfitting words which should be rebukefull or spiteful" against the Portreeve and his council, or to take "any part" against them. For this last the Portreeve could even impose a sentence of imprisonment. Burgesses were not even allowed to let or sub-let part of their property without his agreement.

The status of the Portreeve and Aldermen of the town was further enhanced by certain perks to which they were entitled. Only they were allowed to stop traders on their way to the town market and purchase goods from them "for their own households". When the market opened first they and the rest of the burgesses, as well as "gentlemen for their own household" enjoyed 'first pick' of the wares on sale. Only then it was it thrown open to the rest of the town's inhabitants and folk from the surrounding country.

## *The Seal of Kenfig Borough*

The seal was used by Alice the widow of John Peruat, a former burgess of Kenfig for her gifts of land and two burgages in the town to Margam Abbey in 1320 & 1321 because *"her seal is unknown to many persons"*. In return for the messuages she received a daily pension of a conventual loaf and a gallon of beer from the monks for the rest of her life. [PM198-9] In August 1325 the seal was again used, probably for the same reason, by John the son of John Nichol of Kenfig when he quit-claimed to the monks all his land and burgages in the town. He did rather better from his deal, becoming a free sergeant of the abbey receiving daily a conventual loaf, two loaves known as 'livraisons' (made like a thin open book) and a gallon of beer. This was in addition to a wage of half a silver mark, four pairs of shoes worth twelve pence, a quarter of oats, and pasture for two beasts [PM 200] Of the seal Birch comments that its *"rude simplicity for a flourishing borough... is quite remarkable"*. It was, however not the only seal used by the burgesses. The February following John Nichol's charter, John the son of Henry de Bonville used the Kenfig Borough seal on a receipt for payment in lieu of arrears on a similar pension he was receiving from the monks. Instead of the ornamental cross between four pellets this one (which is damaged) displays the device of a fleur-de-lis.

Throughout the Ordinances the Aldermen are closely associated with the Portreeve and are frequently referred to as his 'brethren'. How a burgess achieved this status is nowhere stated, but in the later Borough they were those who had previously held the office of Portreeve. At that time the status was largely honorary, but it is clear that in medieval Kenfig they formed the Town Council, though this is not to say that they exercised any direct control over the Portreeve himself. As in later times the council's job was only to offer him advice and counsel, but any decisions he made were his own. I can think of quite a few politicians who would dearly love to have such legislation at their disposal today!

However raw and unlikely it might seem, the Kenfig community was a crude democracy, in which democratic values applied. A ruthless holder of the office might have his year as Attila the Hun, but at the end of it he had to stand for re-nomination to the post. Any unpopular or contentious legislation he may have forced through in the teeth of his council's opposition could easily be undone by his successor. As discussed in the next chapter, this simple fact may actually have eventually contributed in a small way to the community's ultimate downfall.

To govern his town and borough the Portreeve could call upon the services of several officers who like himself were appointed annually. Chief amongst them was the Sergeant-at-Mace who traditionally had the care and custody of this symbol of the town's status and bore it before the Portreeve in procession. He was also the latter's 'executive officer' who saw that his instructions were put into force and collected the various duties and rents owed by the inhabitants to both the town and its lord.

To assist the Sergeant there were two Aletasters who were the town's 'Weights and Measures Officers' checking both the quality of the goods and services offered by the town and the measures used by the traders. For this they would have been equipped with a standard set of measures against which those used by merchants and shopkeepers could be checked. There would have been a Kenfig yard; a Kenfig pint; and a Kenfig bushel, for there was invariably a slight discrepancy between such standard units in towns across the country. In the later borough they are also recorded as assisting the Sergeant to collect the rents and rates, and this also probably formed a part of their original duties.

Law enforcement within the town was in the hands of the Petty Constable who was the one Borough officer who did not necessarily have to be a burgess. Like the others he undertook this task alongside his normal employment which he was expected to set aside whenever called upon to fulfil the duties of his office. When a crime occurred then he could deputise anyone, perhaps the entire community (the so-called 'hue and cry') to assist in the capture of the culprit. It occurs to me that there must have been some form of professional or semi-professional 'town watch' to guard the gates by night and help the constable keep order, but no such body finds mention in the records of the time.

The Hayward was responsible for policing the town's common, a job considered of such importance that in the later Borough he was paid a small salary. His main task was to ensure that no 'strange' cattle or other livestock were pastured there, only those belonging to the burgesses. As sand encroachment began to affect the area of the Borough in the 14th century his duties multiplied. He was required to make a daily survey of the common for strays belonging to outsiders, and was also to enforce new legislation forbidding burgesses to pasture cattle under three years of age on it. The regulation that pigs should have rings inserted in their noses when turned out to graze may also have come into being at this time.

An official not mentioned in contemporary documents is the Borough Recorder. He combined the offices of Town Clerk and Treasurer, and it would be impossible to envisage an arm of local government without him even eight centuries ago! Who else would have kept the accounts and records that even a fledgling bureaucracy spawns? To be appointed to this key post a person would have needed to be both literate and numerate, so it is likely that as was later the case they probably held the post for years on end and received some small remuneration for the work.

Together with the Keeper of the Cross whom we met earlier in this chapter these were the officials and leaders of the little community at Kenfig. Sadly we know neither their names nor their deeds, for no such information has survived down to the present day but, together with the Constable of the Castle it was they who were responsible for the safety and well being of their town. No doubt there were heroes and there were villains, and those just doing their incompetent best, but they were all people who played a leading role amongst the Kenfig folk of their day.

# Chapter 9

## THE FINAL ASSAULT

Although the failed attack upon Kenfig in 1232 was the last act in the sustained attempt by the Lords of Avan to secure control of the town and the surrounding district, it was by no means the end of such violence against the community. In 1242, two years after the death of Morgan Gam, his cousin Hywel ap Maredudd of Miskin descended upon the town and once again left it in ruins.

### Hywel ap Maredudd's War

Hywel it will be recalled had captured and mutilated his cousin Morgan ap Cadwallon in 1227, possibly annexing his lordship of Glynrhondda and the Ogmore and Garw Valleys that the latter had also brought under his sway. Then, in 1229 when Morgan Gam was temporarily removed from the scene by Earl Gilbert, he attacked and burnt St Nicholas and St Hilary.

The subsequent release of Morgan Gam may have caused him to curb his activities, but with the latter now in his grave, Hywel seems to have set himself the task of turning Miskin into the leading Welsh lordship in Glamorgan. The attack upon Kenfig apart, he sought to achieve this not by attacking the Lord of Glamorgan (Richard de Clare) head on, but rather at the expense of some of the Earl's leading tenants within the Lordship, both Welsh and Anglo-Norman.

Glynrhondda may, or may not, have been in his hands in 1242, but the Kenfig attack was but a side-show in a larger conflict he was waging against Rhys ap Gryffydd of Senghenydd on the one hand and Gilbert de Turberville of Coity on the other.

The dispute within the latter was probably provoked by Hywel's occupation of Llangeinor and Llandyfodwg (in Glynogwr). Technically these belonged neither to Hywel nor Morgan ap Cadwallon, nor indeed to Turberville, but were part of the former De Londres Manor attached to Ogmore Castle. Its lords, however, were far more concerned with their Marcher Lordship of Kidwelly, and throughout the medieval period seem to have treated these hill territories as something of an embarrassment they could rather do without. The population there was entirely Welsh and generated little income. During the uneasy peace of 1185-1218 land at Llangeinor was turned over to the monks of Margam Abbey who had created a grange there which they later abandoned in the 14th century. About that time, and shortly after the ravages of the Black Death in 1349, there is a record of an enquiry being held into the legal ownership of these uplands 'because the community claimed them'. It is almost as though the complete lack of interest on the part of the Lords of Ogmore had led the inhabitants to believe they were their own rulers!

The fate of Llangeinor and Llandyfodwg were nevertheless of paramount concern to the Turbervilles of Coity whose land bordered it on the south. This northern part of their member lordship is still called 'Coity Wallia' today because from time immemorial (legend claims from the days of the very first Turberville to settle here) this had been a 'Welshry'. Here the family allowed the native population to live according to their own laws and customs unhindered, and it was an arrangement that seems to have worked well. The last thing that Gilbert de Turberville (who was the Lord of Coity in 1242) wanted at this time was somebody like Hywel fomenting trouble amongst these Welsh tenants. By a charter (Birch, 1897: 270) that probably dates from this period he quit-claimed to the Abbot of Margam "all his right in the land of Egleskeynwir [Llangeinor], or to the common of pasture there". This is a very curious statement indeed for, so far as anyone is aware he possessed no legal claim to this land anyway! It seems, in fact, that in the absence of any reaction from the legal owners to the Welsh annexation of this land, he had simply thrown his own hat into the ring as well!

***Coity Castle*** *to the North-East of Bridgend*

What quarrel Hywel had with Rhys ap Gryffydd of Senghenydd I don't know, but it seems to have been one of long standing, for this latest episode was said to be in breach of a previously agreed truce between them.

In an attempt to restore order, a deputation led by the Abbot of Tewkesbury was appointed to look into the causes of this disruption, though what their findings were is not known. They nevertheless imposed a peace settlement upon the warring factions, taking hostages from the Welsh lords and lodging them at Cardiff Castle as sureties for their future good behaviour. Despite this by December 1244 Hywel was again at loggerheads with another of his neighbours, Richard Siward, Lord of Llanblethian, Talyfan, and Ruthin though in this instance it would seem that he was not the instigator of the conflict (Crouch, 1991).

Siward was a violent, unruly and unprincipled character who in the 1230s had displaced the De St Quentin family from these member lordships which they had probably held since Robert FitzHamon's day. He apparently raided Hywel's lands kidnapping several prominent Welsh freemen, thus prompting Hywel to retaliate in kind by capturing a certain Thomas de Hodnet, for whom he demanded a ransom of 200 marks.

A jury of twelve were appointed by Earl Richard de Clare to look into the matter, and he ordered Siward to release the captured Welshmen forthwith as his actions had been in breach of a truce that existed between himself and Hywel (presumably the one arrived at in 1242). Siward simply chose to ignore Earl Richard's order, claiming that the feud was a private matter between himself and Hywel in which neither the Earl nor his commission had any legal right to interfere. Their estates, he claimed, were in fact (if not in name) mini-Marcher Lordships where the Earl had no more right to interfere than the King of England had in the affairs of Glamorgan. The council broke up in confusion.

Hywel and Siward then concluded a private treaty and combined forces to launch an attack upon Earl Richard's property. They caused damage claimed by the latter to amount to over a thousand pounds. When Siward attended a sitting of the County Court on 5th July, 1245 he was therefore arrested and forced to surrender his castle at Talyfan as surety for his appearance at the next sitting to answer a charge of sedition. When he failed to do so, and then did not appear at two subsequent sittings of that court, he was declared an outlaw according to Glamorgan law and custom. On this pretext Earl Richard seized all Siward's Glamorgan estates with the exception of Merthyr Mawr. He likewise ejected Hywel from Miskin, though how exactly this was achieved (and whether it had any legal basis) is not known.

Although Siward began legal actions against the Earl, these petered out following his death in 1248 and neither he, Hywel, nor their descendants succeeded in securing a return to their former properties. Earl Richard in the meantime further secured his hold upon the former territories of his two turbulent lords by establishing borough towns at both Llantrisant and Cowbridge. The latter, which was in being by the year 1254, grew rapidly to become more than double the size of Kenfig, though Llantrisant never flourished to the same extent.

The creation of Cowbridge was important for Kenfig in that it marked a realignment of the Portway – the road linking it to Cardiff - from the meandering track via Llanblethian that had hitherto served the purpose since the days of Robert FitzHamon. A deliberate return was made to the more direct route of the ancient Roman road, and it is perhaps at this time that the ford across the Ogmore river was located near the New Bridge (The Dipping Bridge). This was certainly the main highway in later ages, cutting out the long detour to the ford at Bridgend and it is noticeable that the castles at Newcastle and Oldcastle both went into decline about this time. Notwithstanding the subsequent building of a bridge to link the two settlements, and the creation of Bridgend as a market town the area reverted into something of a backwater of only local importance for nearly 600 years.

## The First Industrial Revolution.

This re-alignment of the main road, which became known as The Portway, was probably inspired and directed by Richard de Clare who also instituted another major development on his Welsh estates that had an effect on Kenfig and district.

It is said that in 1231, during the days of his father Gilbert, mines of silver, lead and iron were located on the De Clare estates in Wales (Clark, 1883: 89), and it seems that Richard now set about developing these resources on a commercial basis. His principal operations were centred upon Trellech in Monmouthshire where archaeologists have discovered the remains of extensive iron working dating from this period. The success of the industry saw this town grow into the largest in Wales though it sank back into obscurity with equal rapidity following the death of the last of the De Clares in 1314.

Echoes of this early but short-lived Industrial Revolution are also found at Kenfig. The Abbot of Margam, for example, was quick off the mark to try and secure some advantage for his community, his interest being indicated in three surviving Abbey charters. One, dated 17th April, 1261 is by a Robert Russel whose property seems to have been in the vicinity of Pen-y-fai (now in Bridgend), and who ceded to the monks the right to any "marl, iron or lead" they could find on his common land (Birch, 1897: 274). Amongst the witnesses to this deed is Phillip de Cornelly who, in another document of about the same date gave the Abbey the rights to any "iron and lead on the east side of the highroad " leading to Newton within his manor of South Cornelly (Birch, 1897: 192). Finally there is an undated charter from an Owain ab Alaythur who belongs to the period 1217-1246 "of all the stony coal on his land and his men's land, with ingress and egress for two-wheeled and four-wheeled carts" (Birch, 1897: 257).

These concessions simply allowed the monks to prospect land that was not actually in their possession, and as such undoubtedly represent a far wider survey on other land that the Abbey actually owned. As much of this was indeed rich in certain minerals it has become virtually an article of faith that the monks located and mined at least some of the coal measures on their property. This, however, is more than the evidence allows. There is, for example, no mention of any profits accruing to the monastery from mining operations either in the Pope Nicholas taxation of 1291 (which lists all the Abbey's sources of revenue) or another return made concerning its sources of income in 1336. The only mention of any actual mining activity is in fact found in documents relating to the dissolution of the monastery when there was a coal works on Abbey land at Cefn Cwsc on the north side of Cefn Cribwr[38]. This mine was certainly not being operated by the monks themselves, but

---

[38] As, for example, in an abstract of property purchased by Rice Mansel, PM 1194.

was either leased to, or otherwise rented by, a lay contractor working for his own profit.

Mines that have been pointed out to me as ones 'once worked by the monks' all appear to belong to a later era, being in the form of levels driven into seams of coal outcropping at the surface. My understanding is that any monastic operations during the medieval period would have been in the form of 'bell pits' which was still the method in use locally when the Cefn Cwsc mines were in operation in the 16th century.

Bell pits developed from shafts sunk at locations where coal measures lay near the surface. At the base of the shaft miners worked the seam outwards in all directions leaving pillars of coal to support the roof thereby creating the characteristic bell shape that gave these early pits their name. The trick, apparently, was to chose the right moment to suspend operations before these inadequate props could no longer support the roof and the whole thing collapsed! When this happened a bowl-shaped depression appeared on the surface, and it is these that mark the location of the former mines at Cefn Cwsc.

Whilst Margam Abbey may therefore never have benefited from the result of its prospecting in the middle of the 13th century, there is some evidence that one or more of the Kenfig burgesses took this sudden interest in the local mineral wealth a stage further.

The excavation carried out by the Kenfig Society (Robbins, 2002) to the west of Kenfig castle has uncovered evidence that operations involving metal working were going on at this spot at about the same time the Abbot of Margam was securing the right to prospect elsewhere in the surrounding district. It was indeed rather a strange operation. The site is well outside the town walls and had already been encroached upon by sand when the work started. Upon it some rather flimsy buildings were erected that are apparently domestic in character. Associated with them, however, are quantities of iron-scale which are flakes that form on the surface of the red-hot metal whilst it is being worked. To date no evidence has been uncovered of the forge at which the work was being done, and by itself the evidence suggests nothing more than the operations of a lone blacksmith.

Nearby, however, our team discovered a pit filled with no less than 48lbs of iron slag that had been buried, along with some bone and pottery fragments. The burial of the slag, and the location of this site amongst the dunes suggest that what was taking place here was possibly a clandestine operation. Was the smith 'testing' the viability of local ore on behalf of the Lord of Kenfig or (and this seems the more likely explanation), was he obtaining his ore from a local mine for which he had not obtained that lord's permission? Either way it seems that the Kenfig burgesses were fully aware of the sudden rush to exploit the mineral wealth of South Wales and were at least dabbling in the operation themselves.

**Alarms & Excursions**

Although we cannot be sure how long the smithing operation in the dunes continued, it is unlikely to have been of any great duration. It lay beyond the shelter of the castle and town walls so the persistent Welsh raids upon the town during the second half of the 13th century would certainly have forced its abandonment.

After the attack of Hywel ap Maredudd in 1242 things seem to have remained tranquil in Glamorgan until July 1256 when an assassination attempt was made upon the life of Richard de Clare. Poison was the chosen method and although he survived, his brother William died and the identity of the murderers apparently never established. The King immediately sent an army to protect Glamorgan, but this was probably no more than a precaution for we hear of no violence erupting within the lordship.

The Earl, who had been abroad when the attempt had been made on his life, was allowed little time to recover. Llewelyn ap Gryffydd of Gwynedd ('Llewelyn the Last') overran Mid Wales the following January and was threatening to invade Kidwelly and

Gower so the King placed Earl Richard in charge of all Royal Forces in South Wales with orders to bring Llewelyn to heel.

Prompted by the Prince's success the Welsh leaders in Carmarthenshire launched a rebellion of their own, winning a notable victory at Cymerau (between Llandeilo and Carmarthen) and followed this up by capturing the castles of Laugharne, Llanstephan and Narberth. Llewelyn and his army then joined the mayhem with raids upon the unpopular Flemish settlements about Rhos and Haverfordwest.

Earl Richard meanwhile was still gathering his forces at the former St Quentin castle of Llanblethian and (for whatever reason) made no immediate attempt to intervene and bring the Welsh to battle. From his spies, moreover, he was probably aware that having ravaged the Flemish settlements, Llewelyn and his army were now marching east towards Glamorgan. This being so he may well have had a plan that he hoped would force the Welsh Prince to accept battle.

Pitched battles were surprisingly rare during the medieval period, and most wars revolved around the siege and capture of the enemy's principal fortresses. As Richard perhaps saw it, Llewelyn would now attack either Neath or Kenfig in an effort to secure a foothold in western Glamorgan. Whilst there was little realistic hope of the actual towns holding out longer than the first assault, the castle garrisons could be expected to put up a sterner resistance, allowing the Earl the opportunity to descend upon Llewelyn's army and force a battle outside the town walls.

But if Richard believed he knew the location and intentions of Llewelyn's army then it seems Llewelyn was fully aware of the location of his opponent's own force. Instead of obliging the Earl by threatening either Neath or Kenfig he made his way through the mountains to the outpost castle at Llangynwyd (near Maesteg) and attacked that instead. In the overall scheme of things it was a totally meaningless victory, but its symbolism would not have been lost upon the Welsh of Glamorgan. Effectively what Llewelyn had done was to thumb his nose at Earl Richard before scuttling off back to Gwynedd leaving Llangynwyd castle in flames that is remembered in the badge of Maesteg and Tir Iarll to this day.

The Prince and his army returned again two years later in 1259, though to the relief of the Kenfig burgesses it was neighbouring Neath that he chose as the object of his attack on this occasion. His visit was again no more than a raid made perhaps with the object of stirring up the local Welsh into a rebellion that would help keep Richard de Clare looking over his shoulder to the security of his own estates. Although Neath town was captured and destroyed, the castle garrison repulsed his attack and rather than getting involved in a regular siege he again withdrew.

The result of the Prince's two raids bore fruit a few years later in 1262 after a second attempt to kill Richard by poisoning met with success. As was the custom an *Inquisition Post Mortem* listing his estates and their sources of income in great detail was drawn up following his death—the earliest one to survive in respect of the Lordship of Glamorgan. This tells us that eighty homesteads had been destroyed in Tir Iarll and that Kenfig mill had been demolished, but makes no mention of the Borough as it was (temporarily) in the hands of a Roger de Clifford. Clearly there had been an uprising in the district, and in view of the destruction of the mill it is very hard to believe the town itself had escaped unscathed. At Neath, which was still recovering from Prince Llewelyn's earlier visit, 150 houses are reported to have been destroyed.

For Kenfig there then followed (or so it would appear from the sparse documentary material available) over thirty years of peace punctuated by occasional threats that apparently never materialised. In 1265 Llewelyn and Simon de Montfort (who was in rebellion against the Crown) were active in Gwent and then launched an attack upon Glamorgan (Earl Gilbert de Clare having sided with the King) which 'they laid waste' (Clark, 1883: 128). From 1266 to 1272 there was constant bickering going on between Prince Llewelyn and Earl Gilbert in the east of Glamorgan following the latter's ejection of the Welsh lord of Senghenydd and the construction of the castle at Caerphilly.

Llewelyn was finally defeated and killed in 1282. Five years later a rebel army led by a certain Rhys ap Maredudd, having captured several castles in West Wales came east to plunder Swansea and burn the fortress at Oystermouth. None of these disturbances, however, seem to have directly affected the lives of the good burgesses of Kenfig.

Their peace was eventually shattered by a local uprising in 1294/5 led by a shadowy figure known only as 'Morgan of Avan'. This was part of a more widespread rebellion which occurred throughout Wales at this time. It is claimed that for a while Morgan succeeded in securing complete mastery of Glamorgan but a lightning campaign launched by King Edward I from Conway in April 1295 swept through Wales and had restored order by the end of June. During the uprising both Kenfig and Llangynwyd castles were attacked and the latter was destroyed, never to be rebuilt. When Earl Gilbert de Clare died in the December of that year the Inquisition carried out on his death shows that the town of Kenfig had still not recovered, rent only being accounted for in respect of thirteen burgages.

Despite the fact that the Welsh Princes had been totally crushed, the uprising of 1295 marks the commencement of what was arguably the most violent phase of Kenfig's history. In 1314, following the death of Gilbert, last of the Clares, at the battle of Bannockburn, the mysterious 'Morgan of Avan' again resurfaced to lead a rebellion, though on this occasion he was captured and despatched to the Tower of London on 7th December. What damage he may have caused at Kenfig is uncertain, but the town and the castle had certainly been attacked for the fortress was defended by none other than the current Lord of Avan and descendant of Morgan Gam named Leision who styled himself 'D'Avene'. He claimed expenses amounting to forty marks for his efforts, but King Edward II maintained that Leision had in effect only been defending his own property (the Avan Lordship), and allowed him just half that amount!

The extent of the damage caused to the town on this occasion is not known, but worse was to follow. Llewelyn ap Gryffydd of Senghenydd (better known simply as Llewelyn Bren) was driven into rebellion by certain injustices heaped upon him by Payn de Turberville of Coity, the King's bailiff for the Lordship. His attempts to secure justice from the Crown drew only an unsympathetic and hostile response, so in January 1316 he attacked and destroyed the town at Caerphilly but was unsuccessful in his attempts to take the castle. For a time the whole of South Wales was in uproar though the rebellion itself was in fact of short duration. Having been defeated in a battle on the slopes of Caerphilly Mountain, Llewelyn and his remaining followers eventually surrendered at Ystradfellte on 16th March.

At Kenfig the accounts of John Giffard covering the period from April to September 1316 (Evans, 1964: 31-2) show that it had received a severe mauling during the unrest. Forty-two out of the town's 142 burgages had been destroyed whilst many holdings in Tir Iarll lay vacant as the tenants (having espoused Llewelyn's cause) had fled. Madoc Vychan, the steward there, was committed to the Tower of London (though he was eventually pardoned) and the Welsh inhabitants fined fifty marks for their part in the uprising, though this too was later remitted. The general uncertainty of the district even after Llewelyn's capitulation is reflected by the employment of a sentinel at Kenfig for 163 days at 2d per day "for fear of war".

This was to be the last known purely Welsh attack upon Kenfig. According to local lore Owain Glyndwr descended upon the town and destroyed the castle in 1405 but, although a possibility, nothing to confirm this claim has ever come to light. The last known attack came in the year 1321 when a mixed Anglo-Norman and Welsh army (including our old friends Leisian D'Avene and Morgan Vychan of Tir Iarll) descended upon the town. They were led by nobles in rebellion against the King and bent upon causing as much damage as possible within Glamorgan because it was part of the estates of his much-hated favourite Hugh le Despenser the Younger. The ease with which this army marched through South Wales capturing and destroying the Despenser castles suggests that few, if any, of the garrisons were disposed to lay down their lives on their lord's behalf. In such circumstances it may well be that Kenfig town itself escaped with little damage.

This, incidentally, is the sole occasion on which the castle at Kenfig is ever known to have fallen to an enemy assault and, also perhaps the last occasion on which the burgesses were required to defend the town walls. Nevertheless, as the rebel army marched away to do their worst to other Despenser fortresses, out to the west Kenfig town was already under attack from a far more powerful and insidious enemy.

**"The ruin of Kenfig castle,**
*from the obscurity of its situation, is rarely visited by strangers. It lies upon a small eminence, surrounded by a cluster of sand hills, in the midst of a sandy plain that stretches along one side of the village"*
*(from Donovan's 1805 Excursions through South Wales )*

# Chapter 10

## ABANDONDED – AND RE-BORN

**The Shifting Sand.**

When and why the town and castle of Kenfig were finally abandoned are questions that have intrigued historians for many centuries. The 'when' will be explored in due course, but suffice is to say here that if one is looking for firm and solid evidence then all we can say is that the town was still in existence in 1397 (the date of its earliest surviving charter), and had gone 140 years later in 1538 when its ruins were seen by John Leland (1549). The simple fact is that no record of its abandonment has survived down to the present time.

The 'why' is likewise not quite as simple as might be expected. Since the entire location where the town and castle stood is covered by sand it seems reasonable to suppose that sand encroachment was the culprit. This in turn opens up a new can of worms. Why and how did the sand move in the first place? Move it certainly did, and along the south bank of the Kenfig River it pushed inland for a distance of nearly two miles!

When I set out on this personal odyssey to write a history of Kenfig I held little hope of ever answering any of these questions, but as my research progressed, so various facts began to emerge from which a reasonable picture of the end of Kenfig could be inferred. One particular theory about the arrival of the sand should perhaps be discounted immediately as it still surfaces from time to time. This is that the sand dune areas of South Wales were the result of a gigantic sandstorm that originated in the Sahara Desert, a theory given a veneer of credibility from the fact that under a microscope, sand grains from Kenfig and elsewhere are indeed identical to those from that great wasteland. That this is so is simply because, whatever their original provenance, both have been blown about by the wind for many hundreds of years wearing away the sharp edges typical of 'sharp' sand from rivers and sea. As we will see, the advance of the Kenfig sands took place over a period of time—not as the result of a single incident. Added to this is the unanswerable question as to why a sandstorm of such proportions should be so selective in the locations that it deposited sand, and why these locations should all be on the coast!

The sandstorm theory is therefore, quite simply, a 'non-starter', but still leaves us with the question of why the sand covered such a vast area. In searching for the answer I was considerably assisted by the work of others who had previously sought an answer to this major conundrum.

Peter Jones was the Deputy Warden and then briefly the Warden of Kenfig Dunes National Nature Reserve. Whilst here he obtained a Doctorate based upon a study of the formation of the dunes with particular reference to the underlying water table. A copy of his thesis is still held at the Dunes Centre (Jones, 1993) though most of what I learnt from him was the result of discussions we had during the course of his research. It was in answering one of his queries as to why the amount of vegetation on the dunes has increased so enormously over the past 40-50 years that I actually stumbled across the major reason why the sands moved in the first place.

I also had the pleasure of meeting Luke Toft on several occasions, though his research on sand movement in the Swansea Bay area is more readily available having been published by the journal *Morgannwg* in 1988. He in turn had built upon earlier work done by Leonard Higgins (1933) of Porthcawl, and whilst I do not necessarily share all Luke's conclusions, the research upon which he based his findings is sound enough.

Our story starts back in the dim and distant past some two thousand years before the birth of Christ. At that time what we today know as Swansea Bay was largely dry land—a comparative term since much of it was salt marsh and brackish pools through which the rivers Tawe, Neath, Afan and Kenfig wended a sluggish course to the sea. That this was so can be demonstrated by the existence of the remains of a 'petrified forest' visible at extremely low tide near Swansea and the layers of peat beneath the beach at Kenfig revealed by recent erosion there. Some remembrance of this land was contained in a local legend (the details of which have long been forgotten) about a lost land lying between Porthcawl and 'Pengwyr' (Worm's Head) (Griffiths & Lyons, 1996: 23-4).

When exactly the sea engulfed this land I cannot tell you, but a sample of peat taken from below the dunes fringing Kenfig Beach in the 1970s showed that it had died (having presumably become covered with sand) about 1700 years before the birth of Christ (Carr, 1975).

The formation of these early dunes would have been the logical consequence of the formation of Swansea Bay so the inundation would presumably have occurred about that time. The waters of the bay are comparatively shallow, which means that in an area with the second highest tidal range in the world, wide tracts of foreshore covered by sand are exposed at low water. Luke Toft in his *Morgannwg* article states that winds of sufficient strength to move dry sand occur locally over about two-thirds of the year. Any such wind blowing onshore was therefore capable of moving sand from the beach above the high-water mark, and at Kenfig the prevailing winds are ones blowing from that direction. – i.e. from the west. It is therefore no surprise that shortly after the creation of Swansea Bay a dune area formed immediately behind the foreshore of Kenfig Beach.

Once above the high-tide level the sand became subject to different conditions than when on the beach. To quote Peter Jones, "Wet sand don't move" (at least, not through wind action!), and the beach is covered by the sea twice every twenty-four hours. The sands of the foreshore dunes are, however, only wet when it rains.

In theory therefore there was nothing to stop the wind rolling them inland unchecked. Peter's research into the water-table beneath Kenfig Dunes showed why (initially at least) this was not the case either here or elsewhere around the margins of Swansea Bay.

The soil that underlies the dunes is boulder clay, which is impervious to water. By blocking the natural drainage of the coastal plain the dunes created areas of marshland and bog on their inland side. The most notable feature of these is the lake at Kenfig Pool. During wet winters much of the low-lying land between the dunes ('slacks') lie flooded for weeks, even months on end. It is a process one can also see at Oxwich in the Gower, and (prior to construction and building work) at Baglan Moors and Crymlyn Bog. 'Wet sand' let me remind you, 'Don't move', so except in prolonged dry spells expansion of the dunes inland was brought to a halt. This in turn allowed vegetation around the fringes of the sand to re colonise any ground lost, and the hardy plants that made their home here likewise impeded further advances both by their very presence and by trapping wind-blown sand in their foliage. It was the partial destruction of this vegetation that subsequently caused the sand at Kenfig to move, and the instrument of that destruction may well have been human interference with the fragile ecology of the dunes[39].

## The Road to Doomsday

An extract from a document of the early 1300s shows us how it all started. In a return of the receipts received for the manor of Kenfig for the period 20th April to 29th September 1316, the bailiff, John Gifford, wrote:

---

[39] My explanation outlined in these notes is at odds with the generally accepted one, advanced by Higgins and Luke Toft, who place the blame squarely on the rising tides and deteriorating climatic conditions. Although these undoubtedly contributed, the argument for them being the only, or even the principal cause of sand encroachment is seriously flawed as set out in Appendix IV.

The same answers for 2 shillings and 6 pence received from a certain pasture which is called Conynger sold for the same time, and there is less because the great part is drowned by the sea.

Thomas Gray, who included this item in his 1909 book on Kenfig (p22), then goes on to point out that in an account submitted two years earlier by Bartholomew de Baddlesmere there were two payments—12 pence (one shilling) and 2s. 6d.—received in respect of "the Conies Pasture" over a period of three months. This amounts to fourteen shillings for the year, whereas the equivalent rent from Giffard's account is just five shillings. From this comparison therefore it would seem that almost two-thirds of the land had been flooded.

The name 'Conyger' indicates a rabbit warren, and the one at Kenfig continued in being until well into the 19th century. It occupied the land nearest to the sea which, as we have seen would have been a relatively narrow tract of foreshore dunes at the time Kenfig town was founded. Giffard and Baddlesmere's accounts show that the warren was evidently being operated on behalf of the Lord of the Manor and also that in order to 'maximise the return' local people were being allowed to pasture livestock there in return for a fee. In time this would become part of the common land freely available to the burgesses for this purpose, but in the 14th century it lay outside the boundary of their Borough.

Dramatic evidence showing the effect of grazing livestock and rabbits on the dunes can be seen in two aerial photographs taken in the second half of the 20th century and on display at the Kenfig Dunes Centre. The first, from the 1940s shows that approximately 40% of the area it covers was open sand. In the second, taken about forty years later, hardly any open areas of sand are visible so that today the staff of the reserve are struggling to preserve by artificial means a habitat for the plants and wildlife which the reserve was created to protect.

Various reasons have been advanced for this change. Some claim that the large sandy areas visible in the first photograph were mainly due to the presence of an American Army camp there during WW2 and the associated military training exercises. This may contain an element of truth, but if the memories of our older inhabitants are to be trusted, these operations did not significantly alter the dunes from what they remember from their youth before the Americans arrived.

Another argument that is also currently fashionable is to blame sand-dredging off the coast. This, it is claimed, has visibly reduced the quantity of sand on Kenfig Beach, and thereby the amount blown inland to maintain the dunes. Whilst as concerned as anyone about the large areas of pebbles that have now replaced sand on Kenfig Beach I cannot see any evidence to support it. Most of the beach is still covered by sand today, and the erosion apparent now was quite negligible on the beach in the early 1970s at a time when the greening of the dunes was already in progress.

There are two events, however, that have occurred during the past 120 years which do seem to have a bearing on the state of the dunes today. (Further details of sand movement in the area, see Appendix IV).

The first of these was the abolition of Kenfig Borough in 1886. Under the terms of the Act of Parliament which brought this about, existing burgesses were allowed to keep many of their old privileges and to appoint one son who would inherit them after their day. Beyond this the office of burgess would not be continued. The right to pasture livestock on the dunes was arguably the most important of these rights, and generations of burgesses had exercised it freely in the past. As the burgesses died out, so the numbers of cattle, sheep and horses pastured here reduced until the practice died out altogether.

The second element that has allowed vegetation to proliferate across the dunes was the demise of the rabbit population due to myxomatosis in the 1950s. Rabbits were introduced into

Britain by the Normans who reared them in regular warrens generally situated on land (like the dunes) that was of little use for anything else. As we have seen such a warren already existed in 1314 and continued until well into the second half of the 19th century. By then other small commercial warrens around the fringes of the common had also appeared. Two of these lay north of Y Plwryn, and the other to the east of The Angel Inn. Another existed at nearby Sker. As the Kenfig Corporation bitterly complained during the late 18th and early 19th centuries, escapees from these warrens were causing havoc throughout the common, and the saga of their attempts to eradicate the nuisance is told in Parts IV & V of this history.

Once the warrens were abandoned as commercial ventures the problem increased. I once mentioned to Ted Davies of Kenfig that there must have been thousands of rabbits here before the war. "Barrie", he replied, "there were **millions** of the b......s!", describing how in early morning the surface of the golf course was literally covered with them. Myxomatosis practically exterminated these, and today there are just two small warrens struggling to survive at isolated locations within the Burrows. If the absence of livestock and rabbits from the dunes has allowed the vegetation there to regenerate so dramatically in such a short space of time, then this in turn illustrates the devastating effect their introduction must have had in the first place.

Things were made worse by abnormally high tides as described by Luke Toft and Leonard Higgins. The flooding of the Conyger is an early instance of this, and is paralleled by the inundation of low-lying pastures and breaches in the sea walls at Neath and Briton Ferry during the same period. These floods got steadily worse, and were due to the approaching conjunction of the sun and moon in 1433, a celestial event that occurs every 1,700 years. Most people are aware that on planet Earth the tides are due to the effect of the gravitational pull of the moon, but they are also effected, to a far lesser extent, by the sun. In the century or so approaching this conjunction, and for a similar period afterwards, Northern Europe experienced a series of abnormally high tides that caused widespread and devastating floods. In 1282 several churches were destroyed by floods on the East Coast of Britain; in 1334 the Humber river rose four feet above the previous known highest level; and in Holland the Zuider Zee came into being as a result of floods in 1395. These are just a few of the examples that could be quoted.

I remember, many years ago, how the sea broke through the coastal dunes at Merthyr Mawr near to the Ogmore estuary and flooded some old gravel pits beyond. The immediate effect was devastating as whole dunes dissolved like children's sandcastles on the beach spreading their debris far and wide, burying the existing vegetation. In this particular area the breach in the foreshore dunes was quickly healed by the action of the wind and waves, and the process of regeneration began almost immediately, though vegetation was still noticeably sparser here when I visited the site just a few years ago.

Already unstable due to over-grazing, the coastal fringe of dunes at Kenfig were ripe for movement both by the sea and, more particularly, by the wind as the coast was hit repeatedly by severe gales during the climatic deterioration of the 14th century.

A second peat sample taken from beneath the sand by Carr (1975) in an area on the north of Kenfig Pool indicates that the dunes had spread inland as far as here by the late 13th century. The excavation the Kenfig Society has been carrying out a little further north tends to suggest a slightly earlier date possibly prior to 1250. This has also confirmed moreover that no sand was present here when the town had been founded a century earlier. In this area immediately south of the river, the dunes penetrated further inland than anywhere else, and this was probably due to the fact that unlike the lands further to the south around Kenfig Pool the earliest dunes did not block the drainage of the hinterland to create areas of wetland. As a later reference to the Blacklaak stream indicates the land here drained northwards toward the river, so the advancing dunes had only to cross the width of these small watercourses.

The flooding of the Conyger in 1316 has already been mentioned, but further indications of the true extent of the problem a little further west in the Manor of Neath as indicated by accounts submitted there by Giffard and his predecessors David Oppedoun (1311-12) and Batholomew de Baddlesmere (1314-15)(Hopkins, 1988). Oppedoun mentions that a 4d rent due from a Robert Fleming and William Yros had been defaulted because their land was "submerged by the sea". Baddlesmere says that he had paid out the sum of £4. 9s. 7d. (a considerable amount in those days) to repair several breaches created in sea walls at Briton Ferry. John Giffard in his turn states that there had been no income from the Lord's meadows at Neath "because they were submerged by the sea except for 15 acres which were mown to provide hay for the constable's horses".

In 1336 the Abbot of Margam complained in a return made to the parent house at Clairvaux (Birch, 1897: 305) that "no small part of the [Abbey's] land adjacent to the shore is subject to inundations which often destroy the crops", adding that he anticipated further losses and expenses under this heading. The site of Kenfig, it should be remembered, was only a little above the point to which normal high tides flowed prior to the building of a weir connected with the steel company a little downstream from the castle. As the conjunction of sun and moon approached ever closer it would be reasonable to suppose that the town itself became vulnerable to flooding.

In 1349 an *Inquisition Post Mortem* drawn up on the death of Hugh le Despenser shows that there were then 144 burgages in the town of Kenfig—the highest number on record—but that year saw the arrival in Wales of the Black Death which was already ravaging England. It is estimated that overall it reduced the population by about a third, and was followed in 1361 by another outbreak that had almost as devastating an effect. It is probably these visitations that account for the reduction of the number of burgages to 106 at the time of Edward le Despenser's death in 1375. This reduction in the population came at a time when the sand had already crossed the Blacklaak and was spreading across the common towards the town. A charter given to the burgesses by the same Edward in 1360 states that this stream "used to run" from the southern water of Kenfig to the northern water, which seems a clear indication that its channel had already been blocked and covered by sand.

Something of the concern (not to say panic!) that was gripping the townsfolk at this time echoes down the centuries in the wording of Borough Ordinance No 50. Although undated we can say with certainty that it was made at a time when the dunes were advancing across the adjoining common, but before the year 1397[40]:

It is ordained that the hayward shall dayly make a diligent view and survey over our common and freedom, and thereby to see that no stranger's cattle nor cattles doe pasture upon our freedom. And also see that noe manner of person or persons whatsoever doe reap any sedges, neither draw nor pull any rootes, nor cutt any furzes in any place whatsoever, nor do any other thing that may be to the ruin, destruction and overthrow of the said burrough nor the inhabitants thereof.

For me one of the most poignant aspects of the final days of Kenfig town is that, as this bye-law illustrates, the inhabitants were fully aware of the danger posed by the advancing dunes and of the measures needed to combat it. They fully understood that preservation of the vegetation of the common was essential yet could not bring themselves to take the logical step of closing it to livestock grazing.

---

[40] This is because it refers to the Borough common (singular) whereas the charter granted the town by Thomas le Despenser in 1397 gave the burgesses a second common and pasture rights on a third.

It is easy to sympathise with the Portreeve and his town council in this. The burgesses relied upon dairy products from their cattle that grazed the common to supplement their food supply. If the Portreeve banned all grazing they would be forced to purchase such things or pay for grazing rights elsewhere. It would hit them where none of us like being hit – in the wallet! An embargo on the use of the common would therefore have to be fought through in the teeth of opposition from most burgesses, perhaps leading to violence, riots, and maybe even the overthrow of the council and their leader. The parallel with our own situation with regard to our increasing use of motor cars in the face of a catastrophic build-up of greenhouse gases is too obvious to need any further comment from me.

Further extracts from various Margam charters chart the rapidly deteriorating climatic situation. In 1383 the Abbot was again complaining that much of its property on the coast had "become unfruitful owing to the inroads of the sea and inundations" (Birch, 1897: 319-20). Twelve months later (Clark, 1910) he was bemoaning the fact that because of the floods the Abbey's "pastures and its beasts have suffered beyond hope of improvement". Its buildings, he adds elsewhere (Birch, 1897: 321), were also in disrepair, "dilapidated by the dreadful and unseasonable gales". In 1395 occurred the terrible storm in which the sea breached the coastal defences of Holland creating the vast lake there known as the Zuider Zee that was only reclaimed from the ocean in the 20th century.

Whilst the sufferings of the Abbot and his monks are eloquently expressed in their charters, there are no similar records telling us of the situation at Kenfig. That things here were pretty grim however is implied in the charter granted to the town by Earl Thomas le Despenser in 1397 (Gray, 1909: 108-). He confirmed in full the provisions of the earlier charter given to the town by his father in 1360, and added some bequests of his own. The burgesses were given two new commons outside the Borough boundaries. One lay at 'le Rugge' on the northern side of the western tip of Cefn Cribwr ridge; the other was closer to the town, lying on Kenfig Down between the Pool and the boundary with the Abbot of Neath's grange at Sker. In addition he gave them "one hundred perticas" (about 20 acres) of land adjoining the chapel of Saint Mary Magdalene.

In this way their feudal lord sought to compensate the burgesses for land, both common and arable they had already lost to the sand. His generosity also gave the townsfolk the option of closing down the commons surrounding the town but—the new commons **were** some distance away and—The nett result is that nothing was done and doomsday for Kenfig drew ever nearer.

Previously this charter (in 1397) was the last reliable documentary reference indicating that the town was still in existence. Thomas Gray (1909: 66) found mention of the provisioning of a castle at "Kenflyc" against the Glyndwr uprising in 1405, but this is now believed to be a reference to the one at Cefnllys.

That same year "the castle and town of Kenfeg with the lordship of Tir Iarll" was committed to the custody of Joan the wife of King Henry IV during the minority of Richard le Despenser. This perhaps is a better indication of their continued existence, but beyond that – nothing. There are, it is true, several references to a "town and borough" of Kenfig, but this was a title that continued to be applied long after the medieval town is known to have been abandoned. Similarly, reference to a 'Sir' John Tudur as Vicar of Kenfig in 1411 is equally meaningless as, although the church could have already been abandoned at that time the parish would still have remained in existence.

However, because we now realise that the medieval borough was a smaller entity than the one that replaced it other evidence that was previously of dubious value now provides positive confirmation that the life of the town did indeed extend beyond 1405. Alongside the Thomas le Despenser charter of 1397 the burgesses preserved two others given them by his successors. One is by Richard, Earl of Worcester dated 1st May 1421, and the other (also dated 1st May) was granted by his Countess two years later. In themselves they are of no great interest, merely confirming the provisions of the 1397 charter without reciting the details. The fact they were granted is nevertheless in itself of considerable significance for they confirm that the boundaries of the Borough were still those of 1360.

To obtain these charters the Corporation would have paid, and paid handsomely, but the rights and privileges confirmed by them to the burgesses applied **only so long as they lived within these boundaries**. Had they still not been living in the old town obtaining these confirmations would have been a meaningless (and expensive) exercise. We can therefore be certain that in 1423 the town was still in being, and there is another indication that it was still there nine years later.

This is neither as certain nor as obvious as the evidence provided by the two confirmation charters. It occurs indeed in a document that no longer exists, but is referred to by a Thomas Wyseman during the course of his investigation into a boundary dispute between the burgesses and Jenkin Turberville of Sker in 1592 (PM 9616). Dated to the 9th year of the reign of King Henry VI (1431-2) it contained a reference to the payment of an allowance by the Lord of Glamorgan to a John Stradling as "haywarde & keeper of the Barowes & the Rugge" at Kenfig.

Once the Borough was expanded to its later size the 'Barowes' were included within its boundaries, and became the responsibility of the Hayward appointed by the burgesses. In 1431 this was clearly not the case so it seems therefore that the old borough was still in being; the town still in existence.

Beyond this point nothing is certain, but it seems reasonable to suppose that the Borough boundaries were enlarged either at the time the town was abandoned by the burgesses or very shortly afterwards. This would have been essential for the burgesses to retain their status, for as already mentioned, by moving outside the limits of the medieval borough they effectively disenfranchised themselves.

There are several curious facts about this new successor Borough of Kenfig which (or so I believe) give vital clues to the final days of the old town. The first is that the burgesses did not apparently receive a charter confirming the new boundaries. Had they done so it would undoubtedly have been preserved with the same care as those already in their possession.

Secondly there is the curious fact that the new borough was not confined to land south of the river in the ancient manor of Kenfig that had evolved out of the former 'territory' of that name. Instead it extended across the river - northwards almost to Eglwys Nunnydd on Water Street, and eastwards to include much of the land of the Abbey grange called St Michael's (Llanmihangel). All this was the property of the Abbot of Margam, and this in turn begs the questions, why was such an expansion into land outside the control of the Lord of Kenfig considered necessary, and why did the Abbot consent to it?

## Kenfig Abandoned

In seeking to answer these questions I have evolved a possible theory that I believe answers the final part of our puzzle as to when, and how the town of Kenfig was abandoned. Its subsequent transformation into a new and enlarged 'Second' Borough will be dealt with more fully in Part II of this history. Here I am concerned only with the answers to these two questions.

It is clear from later records that the land of the Borough north of the river subsequently became a regular manor belonging to the Abbey that the monks referred to (very confusingly!) as the Manor of Kenfig. Later still it was known as Higher Kenfig, a name that was applied both to the manor and to this particular portion of the Borough. To avoid confusion between the two Kenfig manors I will therefore refer to it as such in these notes even though technically it is incorrect.

The first mention of this manor comes in an Abbey document dated 1459 (Birch, 1897: 347) which is an extract from its court roll recording the admission of one Jeuan ap Gryffyth as tenant of a property called Gebon ys londe. Gibbons Land was indeed a holding within the later manor of Higher Kenfig, so it is clear that it was in existence at that time. Previously nothing existed here except some outlying elements of St Michael's Grange, and indeed in 1344 the Abbot of Margam had considered turning all the land west of the main road into a rabbit warren. The creation of this Manor of (Higher) Kenfig in the 15th century suggests that it occurred hand in glove with the enlargement of the Borough boundaries across the river. From this therefore we can say that the old town of Kenfig probably went out of existence sometime during the 28 years between 1431 and 1459.

Within that period there arose a set of circumstances that seem to fit the peculiarities inherent in the enlargement of the borough's boundaries very well. On 30th April 1439 Richard Beauchamp, Earl of Warwick, Lord of Glamorgan (and hence Lord of Kenfig) died leaving as his sole male heir a fourteen year old son named Henry. Since the latter was clearly too young to manage his own affairs King Henry VI as his feudal overlord became responsible for the management of his estates. This was a time when the destruction caused by abnormally high tides, as indicated by the Margam charters, was reaching its zenith. An Abbey charter from the following year (Birch, 1897: 342-3) claims that its land was being devastated by "inundations of the sea for upwards of four miles". Given Kenfig's location and the fact that by now the sands had probably reached the edges of the town, such floods would have been devastating. This is echoed in the description of the ruins seen by John Leland (1549) on his visit here a century later in 1538.

There is a litle Village on the Est side of Kenfik and a Castell, booth in ruine and almost shokid and devourid with the sandes that the Severn Se ther castith up

**The site of Kenfig Town today.**
*Much of the dunes are now covered by coarse vegetation due to the lack of over-grazing by livestock and rabbits*

Leland presumably obtained his information from local people when he visited the area a century after the death of Earl Richard. They were the descendants of the former inhabitants, and the memory that the sea played a role in be-sanding the town would have been handed down to them by their grandparents and great-grandparents. Floods would have washed sand from the dunes immediately adjoining the town into its perimeter ditch and the castle moat. It would have swept it down the streets and into the houses, blocking the drains that were the burgesses' primitive sewerage system. Every time the inhabitants attempted to return, clean up the mess, and resume their lives, another flood followed. Sand and sea – it was an irresistible combination.

Descriptions of Kenfig's destruction by other writers in the Tudor period confirm John Leland's account. "A borough town, sometime of good account, but long since decayed by the overflowing of the sand" wrote Rees Merrick (1578). "Drowned within the sande" says Thomas Wyseman (in 1592 from PM 9616), "as maye apere by a parte of the olde church & castle nowe apperynge above the sande".

Whilst the sand remained as the most obvious culprit, none of these writers claim it was brought by sandstorms, and Leland, earliest of the three, specifically mentions that the sea played a major role. This also seems to be confirmed by the reaction of the burgesses to the event. If the dunes merely advanced steadily across the town driving all before them one might expect an equally steady withdrawal of population ahead of them with the town gradually moving eastwards away from its original site. Instead what seems to have happened is that in a relatively short space of time the burgesses moved to new settlements on higher ground north and south of the river - one around Mawdlam church; the other on Water Street. Their reaction is typical of what one might expect in the event of persistent floods "up to four miles inland".

The removal to high ground north of the river is particularly striking, for those who took refuge there chose a location that was not within the jurisdiction of the Lord to whom traditionally they would have looked for succour. Instead it was on land owned by the monks of Margam who these refugees presumably reckoned were a better and more immediate source of aid because of the Abbey's avowed commitment to works of charity.

After one flood too many it seems that the burgesses decided that on this occasion there would be no attempt to return. Having arrived at that decision their next step would have been to inform their Lord of their predicament. It is the subsequent arrangements made by whoever was the effective Lord of the manor at the time that has convinced me that the abandonment was made about the time of the death of Earl Richard Beauchamp in 1439.

When the burgesses moved to either Water Street or Mawdlam the Borough of Kenfig effectively ceased to exist as anything more that a plot of land on the south side of the river Kenfig. The rights and privileges enjoyed by the burgesses ceased to exist; their organisation no longer had any legal right to continue. Had there still been an effective Lord of Kenfig, then within a short space of time a new borough would have been reconstituted either about Heol Las and Mawdlam, or further inland at Pyle. This was not the case, and neither was any charter issued to the burgesses confirming the new boundaries that now came into being. All that happened was that the original Borough was extended north and south of the river to encompass the main areas where the burgesses had taken refuge and their common land at Kenfig Down which had previously been outside the franchise. It seems, in short, to have been a temporary measure designed to keep the Borough organisation in being whilst a more permanent solution was worked out.

This in turn suggests to me that it was a measure taken when there was effectively no Lord of Glamorgan, which was the case after the death of Richard Beauchamp. King Henry and his advisors may have reasoned that by so doing they could safely leave matters in abeyance for young Henry Beauchamp to make his own decision when he reached the age of 21. In this connection I feel that a charter of the King issued in favour of the monks at Margam in 1440 is particularly relevant.

It may well have suited the King and young Henry's trustees to allow part of Kenfig's former population to remain on the Abbey lands north of the river where the monks would care for them. The Abbot of Margam for his part, may well (as we will see in due course) have welcomed the new arrivals for reasons of his own, but would not have been too enamoured to see them reconstituted, even temporarily, as an element of a new borough organisation. This would effectively mean him relinquishing all control over them and the land upon which the huts and shelters they had erected stood.

These would become 'burgess plots'; and the refugees would retain their status as free men.

The King, for his part, had no power to compel the monks to accept his arrangements, so a compromise was arrived at and, not to put too fine a point upon it, he offered a bribe to persuade the Abbot to accept. This was the restitution to the Abbey of their former grange at Llangeinor.

That establishment has already found mention earlier in this chapter. Originally founded on land given to the monks by the De Londres family during the uneasy peace of 1185-1218 it had suffered greatly during the renewal of the war between Earl Gilbert de Clare and Morgan Gam. Although in the 1230s the latter helped the Abbot to secure his title to the land against the local inhabitants, it probably suffered further in the subsequent bickering between Hywel ap Maredudd of Miskin and Gilbert de Turberville of Coity. It was always a difficult area because the hold upon it by the Lords of Ogmore was so tenuous. As previously mentioned, following the Black Death (1349) an enquiry had to be held into their title to the lands of Llangeinor and Llandyfodwg 'because the community claimed it'. By then the monks had already had enough and left. Unable or unwilling to keep up the rent payments due upon the grange the Abbot of the day allowed the property to revert to the Lord of Ogmore in 1337 (Birch, 1897: 342).

Now, over a century later, in 1440 King Henry VI in his capacity as Lord of the Duchy of Lancaster to which Ogmore belonged suddenly restored this property to the Abbey at an annual rent of forty shillings (£2). He says in his charter (Birch, 1897: 342) that his generosity was prompted by the injuries caused to the community during the Glyndwr rebellion and (as mentioned earlier), flooding by the sea up to four miles inland. The latter, as we have seen, is a quite feasible reason, but the Glyndwr rebellion in Glamorgan had been crushed 35 years previously! I would suggest that the monarch was casting about for excuses to cover the real reason which was that this was a bribe to induce the Abbot to allow the refugee burgesses to remain on his land and be included within the boundaries of a new Borough of Kenfig.

The Abbot, for his part, also imposed conditions of his own. Most of his land where the burgesses of Kenfig had taken refuge was undeveloped waste. In the south, on the east side of Water Street, there was some land that had formerly been in cultivation as part of St Michael's Grange (Llanmihangel), but in common with other Abbey Granges this had undoubtedly fallen into decay by this time. (Farm Vach, which lay in this area, is described as having formerly been part of the grange in later documents.) He proposed to allow the burgesses to create small farms for themselves which would make them self-sufficient in the way of food and thereby reduce the drain upon the Abbey's resources. For these, he insisted, they would pay a fair and proper rent. As such therefore they became his tenants and thereby lost their status as free men. Whilst retaining their title and rights as burgesses they could effectively be disfranchised as burgesses if he as their landlord decided to terminate their tenancy agreement. Technically there is no such thing as an 'un-free' burgess, but that is what they were. If, however, as I have suggested this was only envisaged as a temporary arrangement, nobody probably minded too much at the time. These new tenancies were then organised by the monks into a regular feudal manor that was later known as Higher Kenfig.

King Henry's 'temporary solution' to the question of the abandonment of Kenfig was, however, fated to become permanent. Young Henry Beauchamp no sooner reached the age of twenty-one than he died, leaving as his sole heir a baby daughter who followed him to the grave a few years later. Eventually his estates and the Earldom of Warwick were settled upon Richard Neville who, from his frequent changes of side during the Wars of the Roses earned the nickname 'Warwick the King-maker'. In Part II we will see that there is evidence that he did indeed attempt to reconstitute the borough at a new location, but that this was thwarted by his untimely death at the battle of Barnet in 1471. After that, no serious attempt to address the situation seems to have been made and eventually the true origins of the Second Borough with its unusual and perhaps unique quota of 'un-free burgesses' became lost in time.

Meanwhile back at the site of the old town it seems that for a time the burgesses continued to hold onto the ruined burgages they had abandoned, gradually stripping them of all usable timber, stone and thatch to build their new homes. Initially indeed possession of such a plot may still have been essential to anyone aspiring to the status of burgess as is also explained in Part II.

As the winds blew and the dunes advanced across the site covering the ruins of the castle and their former homes, it must have been apparent to even the greatest optimists amongst the burgesses that the three hundred year history of the town had finally come to an end.

# APPENDIXES

# APPENDIX I

# Where was Kenfig 'Old Castle'?

The existence of an 'old castle' somewhere in the vicinity of Kenfig is attested in several documents belonging to the early part of the 13th century. By an undated charter from this period (Birch, 1897: 29), for example, David son of Wasmer rented from the Abbot of Margam five acres of land 'partly lying at Le Horeston on the west of the road which leads to the town of Corneli, and partly under the **old castle'**. The only document that gives some indication where this former castle stood, however, is one by Margery the daughter of Roger which can be dated to the decade 1250-60 (Birch, 1897: 152-3).

Margery was the former wife of Richard the Priest of Kenfig, and because the Roman Catholic Church did not allow its clergy to marry, many writers refer to her as Richard's 'concubine'. The Celtic Church, however, held no such inhibitions regarding married priests. Although suppressed by the Normans and its Abbeys closed down, locally some of its practises seem to have survived. This is by no means the only example of a Roman Catholic cleric in 12th and 13th century Glamorgan taking a wife and raising a family.

By her charter, Margery gave the Abbey of Margam three acres of land split into two adjacent plots described in great detail. One and a quarter acres lay on the western side of a road "from the old castle to Corneli". Another acre and a quarter began "at the said road and lie along to the west as far as the high road leading from Saint Mary Magdalen's Chapel to Corneli".

The road connecting the chapel of Saint Mary Magdalene at what is now Mawdlam village to Cornelly is evidently Heol Las.On the tithe map of 1846 two tithe-free fields are indicated here associated with the tithe barn on the northern side of this road in an area that is now playing fields near Cornelly Cross. These fields arched northwards towards Heol Fach just as the charter describes.

Both were then owned by the Margam estate which was the heir to most of the former monastic property in the area, and in the time of the monks the Abbey had been excused from paying tithes on its land under a Bull issued by Pope Urban III in 1186 (Birch, 1897: 58).

From this it seems clear that the road leading to the 'old castle' was the present high-way to Margam called Heol Fach. Margery's final half-acre, incidentally, is described as lying on the east side of the same road, and in the 17th century the Margam estate had an acre of land somewhere in this vicinity known as Erw Cicily.

Although not providing us with the exact location of the 'old castle', Margery's deed quite clearly indicates that this road led towards it, though no trace of any earthworks that might be those of either a prehistoric or Norman fortification are apparent today. Documentary sources do, however, suggest a strong contender on the ridge known as Mont Mawr which is crossed by the Margam road.

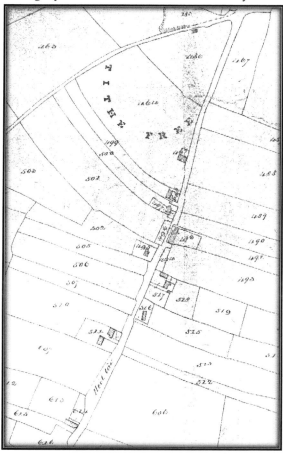

**Map 5: Tithe map of 1846**

The old name for this ridge is 'Mill Hill' which is a shortened version of 'Windmill Hill'. The windmill itself is mentioned in the survey of the Manor of Kenfig Borough in 1570 (PM 9616) when it was already in ruin due to the advancing sand. As Leslie Evans (1964: 34) tells us the mill (and an associated hamlet later known as Millhill) are referred to in the Inquisition Post Mortem carried out on the death of Edward le Despenser in 1375 which mentions pasture at Milmote and Mullhamme. The mill itself is not mentioned as it was almost certainly in private hands at this time.

'Milmote' indicates that this windmill was a typical post-mill of the period mounted on an artificial mound. Today such mounds are virtually indistinguishable from the typical mottes of 12th century castles, so there is a strong possibility that this was originally just such a motte (and the 'old castle' of the charters) which was later re-used for the mill.

There is no obvious trace of such a motte on the ridge today. Not surprisingly the presence of the overgrown dunes here makes it impossible to be sure which (if any) of several likely looking mounds are artificial, and which are merely composed of sand.

When Mr D. Edwards visited this area in 1957 to make an inventory of Archaeological sites on behalf of the Ordnance Survey[41] he was shown one particular spot on the ridge by Mr Dan Rees one of the last surviving burgesses. "This mound", Mr Rees told him, "is known as Twmpath y Felinwynt, and is traditionally the site of a windmill. Celebration bonfires have been lit here since at least 1902. My mother-in-law said the sand swept over the hill about 1877".

Mr Edwards was very dubious about his claim, describing the mound he was shown as "an irregular mound oriented NE – SW with measurements of 24m x 20m, and a height of 0.8m. It is crossed by a sunken NE-SW footpath. It is doubtful if it is the remains of a windmill stead as it appears to be composed entirely of sand and is in an area over which sand has swept".

---

[41]Original index and notes at Bridgend Library

The Inspector was apparently unaware of the documentary evidence confirming the existence of the mill motte which, unless it was removed in the building of the M4 motorway, is there still. Perhaps one day it will be located and excavated to see if it did indeed originate as a 12th century castle.

# APPENDIX II

## The 'Port' of Kenfig

The question of whether or not there ever was a port of Kenfig is one that has earned me no little hassle and a great deal of pleasure. Its existence is assumed almost as a matter of faith, so my own grave doubts about it ever having existed are usually viewed as being somewhat heretical!

Those who base their argument for such a port connecting Kenfig with other havens in the Bristol Channel have indeed got some evidence to support their claim, though in my view much of it is flawed. At the same time I always get the feeling that, be they fellow members of the Society or academics, in part their assumption is that since Kenfig was close to the coast so a port of some sort **must** have existed. This immediately brushes aside the fact that there were coasts, and there were coasts. Some provided safe havens for shipping whilst others (and Kenfig certainly falls into the latter category) were notorious for being the graveyard of such vessels.

The beach at Kenfig is nothing more than an exposed stretch of sand that faces west towards the direction of the prevailing wind. As such for most days of the year it is a 'lee shore' where the wind blows from the sea onto the land, thus making it unsuitable for vessels to land upon since they cannot get off again so long as the wind stays in that direction. Even rowing a small vessel from the beach would have been extremely difficult. If a storm blows up then the boat is trapped on the sand at the mercy of the breakers. What these could do to such a vessel is graphically described in the chapter relating to the wreck of the sailing ship *Mary* of Tenerife which will be dealt with in Part III of this series.

Many I have spoken with accept the validity of this argument but point out that the estuary of the Kenfig River could have afforded some shelter. The question of a port, either in the estuary or a little further upstream is one I will address in greater detail later in these notes. At this juncture, however, let me just point out that the Kenfig is a very small stream and even in the days before the sand began to move inland entered Swansea Bay through a dune system that had been in existence since prehistoric times. It is likely therefore that the entrance to this river was always a difficult one because of constantly shifting sand-bars.

The evidence FOR there being a port at Kenfig can be summarised as follows:

1. 'We have granted also to our aforesaid burgesses that of all merchandise coming to or passing through the aforementioned vill **as well by land as by water** an inspection shall first be made by our aforesaid constable [of the castle] or the provost [portreeve]'.

This extract is from the charter issued to the Borough of Kenfig by Thomas le Despenser in 1397 (Gray, 1909: 109), which in turn is a transcript of another issued to the town by his father Edward in 1360. On the face of it this is clear evidence for vessels bringing goods into the Borough by water, but there is actually some very strong evidence that there was no port at Kenfig at the time these charters were issued.

This negative evidence comes in the form of the absence of any mention of dues being paid to the Lords of Glamorgan at this time in their Inquisitions Post Mortem. These were drawn up on the death of the lord listing the various sources of income due to him from his estates. The earliest one is that of Richard de Clare in 1262 whereafter most of those relating to succeeding lords have survived. These show dues paid from such minor ports as Sully, Llantwit Major and Ogmore-by-sea, but there is no mention whatsoever of any being paid by one at Kenfig. Since (with the exception of Richard de Clare) these lords were all lords of Kenfig, such an absence is surely significant.

My own belief is that this phrase was included in the charter simply because Kenfig was close to the sea and was intended to cover any occasional visits by merchant ships or the possible subsequent development of a haven at this location.

2.    And in delivery of 24 ships which bore the king's timber from Striguil [Chepstow] for the work of the Castle of Kenfig £4. 8s. 3d. by the King's writ. (Gray, 1909: 146)

This again seems, at face value to indicate that if there was no port at Kenfig in the 13th and 14th centuries, then there was certainly one here at the time of this entry in the 'Pipe Rolls' (1184-5).

It relates to a time when the Welsh of South-East Wales were in rebellion and damage had been caused to the castle at Kenfig following two attacks upon the town in just over a year. The first point to be made, however, is that the entry does **not** state that the

*The former course of the Kenfig River as it passed Kenfig Castle*

ships were hired to carry their cargo to Kenfig itself but only to ship timber for which this was the ultimate destination. There is a subtle difference. If the entry had read *'for delivery to Kenfig for the work on the castle there'* or something similar then it would have been unequivocal. As it stands it could mean that it was shipped to a nearby port (such as Newton or Ogmore) to be hauled to Kenfig overland.

The second point about the entry is that it clearly relates to an emergency situation. Normally one would have expected materials for repairs at Kenfig to be obtained locally, from inside the Lordship of Glamorgan. That timber was being brought from as far away as Chepstow is in itself an indication of the turmoil within the lordship. Elsewhere in this history it will be seen that although Kenfig itself held out, the Welsh under Morgan ap Caradoc of Avan had taken possession of Newcastle and much of the intervening territory, so the town was cut-off from the rest of the lordship. It was an emergency situation that required drastic measures and so even if the vessels did indeed land the timber on the coast at Kenfig this in no way implies its regular use as a port.

**3.** For hire of 1 boat for carrying 6 quarters 2 bushels of oats from Kneg' as far as the castle by water in aid of the war, 4d. (Hopkins, 1988: 74)

The two documentary references quoted previously were sufficient to convince Thomas Gray that Kenfig was indeed the location of a port. This possible mention I came across in Anthony Hopkins 1988 *Medieval Neath*. It occurs in the accounts of Gwenllian the widow of Pagan Turberville in respect of Neath town and castle for the winter of 1315-16, and the phrase "in aid of the war" shows that it was made in an emergency situation similar to the one of 1183-5. Neath had in fact been cut off during this rebellion and Gwenllian's husband had died at this time, perhaps as a result of enemy action as her accounts also mention the cost of repairing a breach in the castle walls.

This entry indicates that any port of Kenfig would have been situated within the Borough town itself since this was the area to which the authority of the 'Provost' or Portreeve was confined. As we now know the boundaries of the medieval borough did not extend as far as the Kenfig estuary and the coast but only to the confluence with a stream called the Blaklaak which was probably the out-fall from Kenfig Pool. The river Kenfig is a very small stream, and even allowing for the fact that normal high tides may have reached inland as far as the town, it would have been a very narrow waterway and unlikely to have been sufficiently wide for two vessels to pass one another.

4. The title Portreeve contains the word 'port'.

The title 'Portreeve' cannot be taken as an indication of a 'port' as the original  old English meaning of this word was 'trading centre' rather than a harbour. There was a Portreeve at the later borough town of Llantrisant, though so far as I am aware there has never been a suggestion that this was ever a haven for shipping!

The above therefore is a summary of the evidence that points towards there having been a port at Kenfig, but in my view all three are flawed in some way. Even if the 24 ships from Kenfig actually made their delivery direct to Kenfig, and it is indeed the *'Kneg'* in Gwenllian's account, both occurred in emergency situations where risks perhaps needed to be taken. They do not necessarily imply a commercial haven visited by merchant shipping on a regular basis. In this connection the absence of any dues paid in respect of a Port of Kenfig in the various Inquisitions Post Mortem of the Lords of Glamorgan is particularly damning and negates the suggestion in the town's charter that goods were arriving there 'by water' in the 14th century.

Fellow members of the Kenfig Society with whom I have discussed the question of the port have argued that perhaps in the past the estuary itself extended further inland, citing evidence of a pebble bank lying between the site of the town and the present estuary. They also point out that medieval vessels would have been quite small, but then (I argue in return) size is relative. The ships of the coasting trade that used Newton harbour in the 17th century were classed as 'small', but this was in comparison with larger ocean-going craft. They were still rated at between twelve to thirty tons, so they were no mere rowing-boats.

The fact that the Borough of Kenfig did not actually extend to the sea is, I believe, a particularly significant piece of negative evidence. There were two other borough towns in the Lordship of Glamorgan that were undeniably ports—Cardiff (founded circa 1093) and Neath (founded circa 1129). Like Kenfig both were situated on rivers some distance inland from the coast (perhaps because of the prevalence of piracy in the Bristol Channel). But there was a significant difference: although the main area of land contained within the borough boundaries

*Impression of a seal found by the late Gerrard LaHive at Margam depicting a sailing ship – probably 16th century.*
Photo by Gerrard LaHive

lay around the towns themselves both had a narrow salient extending from it down to the coast alongside of the river. In the case of Cardiff this was land later used for docks, whilst at Neath it became the site of Briton Ferry and its associated harbour facilities.

Why, exactly, this should be the case is not known, but it clearly has something to do with the fact that the rivers Taff and Neath were navigable as far as the town wharves. There was no such extension alongside the river at Kenfig.

Our Society's excavations near the castle at Kenfig have shown that beyond doubt pottery from the Bristol and the West Country was reaching the town throughout the medieval period and logically (given the general state of the roads) this will have been shipped across the Bristol Channel by boat. For all the reasons outlined above, however, I cannot accept that it was shipped directly to a quay in the town itself, but was most likely landed at nearby Newton and brought overland. The earliest evidence of a port here only dates from the early 16th century, but it was already well established and had clearly been there for some time. Because it belonged to the Lord of Newton manor it would not be listed in the *Inquisitions Post Mortem* of the Lords of Glamorgan. My friends in the Society sometimes tease me that one day they'll uncover the remains of a wharf on the banks of the river. If and when they do, then I'll be truly delighted to admit that I'm wrong, but until that happy day I'll cheerfully remain a sceptic!

# APPENDIX III:

## The Blaklaak, an 'Uphill' River

In its report on the early castles of Glamorgan, the Royal Commission on Ancient and Historical Monuments (RCAHMW, 1991: 314-26) includes an extensive section on the remains at Kenfig. Sadly it also contains several flaws, one of the most blatant of which is the statement that the river Kenfig turned southwards at the castle, flowed down through what is now Kenfig Pool, and reached the sea in the vicinity of Sker Point.

To be fair the writer was basing this on the conclusions drawn by somebody else (North, 1957) who noticed that the underwater contours on the Admiralty chart for Swansea Bay seems to indicate the existence of a former estuary at Sker. Noting the existence of Kenfig Pool he therefore, so to speak, simply joined the dots. It is a theory that looks good on a map, and (because of the presence of the dunes) is difficult to argue against on the ground, but it is most certainly incorrect.

The simple fact of the matter is that the pool stands at a slightly higher level than the river, and this was also the case in the medieval period — their relative height above sea-level not having been altered in any way by the influx of the sand. This height difference is only about ten feet, perhaps less, and certainly not sufficiently great to be shown on Ordinance Survey maps, but it is there. This fact was confirmed for me by the late Eiryn Thomas of Tower Cottage, Pyle following a discussion amongst several Kenfig Society members about the feasibility of the allegation made in the Commission's report. When I expressed the view that to have followed such a course it would have actually flowed uphill from the castle to the pool, Mr Thomas was able to confirm this:

In the 1960s the Steel Works at Port Talbot had looked at the possibility of utilising Kenfig Pool as an emergency water supply in the event of drought. This entailed laying a pipeline between the two and Mr Thomas was one of the engineers engaged on this task. They discovered (rather to their surprise I gather) that it would not be necessary to install pumping equipment at the pool. This was because it stood at a slightly higher level than the river, so a simple siphon would be just as effective. The plan was never implemented, and the artificial lake at Eglwys Nunnydd was created instead. Mr Thomas thought that the necessary documents and plans were in the possession of British Steel who were then operating the site at Port Talbot.

I had also contested the theory about the course of the river on historical grounds. A stream called the Blaklaak formed the western boundary of medieval Kenfig Borough. It is mentioned in the earliest document relating to the town – the charter of Robert, Earl of Gloucester pre 1147 – and more interestingly in the town's charter of 1397. In this it appears in a recitation of the borough boundaries copied from an earlier charter of 1360. Speaking of the Blaklaak it states that it "used to run from the southern water to the northern water of Kenfeg". This is taken to mean that it flowed from Kenfig Pool to Kenfig River, but that it had ceased to flow, almost certainly because of the sand incursion. Be this as it may, what cannot be argued with is that this stream had flowed into the Kenfig from the south, and any river flowing in the opposite direction would have been going uphill!

# APPENDIX IV

# The Sand Dune Areas Adjoining Swansea Bay

Between the Ogmore estuary and Rhossili extensive areas of sand dunes have built up at several locations, and in most cases can be shown to have adjoined Norman settlements dating from the 12th century. The history of **Pennard** in the Gower in fact virtually parallels that of Kenfig in this respect. Here there existed a community founded about half a century before Kenfig that also comprised a church, castle and a village. The present remains of the castle (which actually stands on a cliff above the site of the settlement) are dated to about 1270 on architectural grounds. It is mentioned as late as 1350, whilst the church on the lower ground was certainly still in existence in 1291 (Higgins, 1933: 30).

By 1528 the church, its glebe land, and the property of many of the tenants are described as "utterly and clearly destroyed and overdone with the drift sands of the sea", and the entire community had been moved to its present location. Of the castle, a manorial survey of 1650 says that despite its lofty situation "scarcely there remayneth one whole wall" and that it was "now compassed with much sand".

In 1317 when William de Braose as Lord of the Manor granted hunting rights here to his huntsman he specifically excluded his rabbit warren in the sand dunes (RCAHMW, 1991: 289) showing that both dunes and rabbits were present at this location at that time. Furthermore, in 1583 the older inhabitants maintained that they had formerly enjoyed common rights on the land that was then covered by the sand (Higgins, 1933: 31). As at Kenfig, it seems that the original dune system was the location of both a rabbit warren and common pasture for the villager's livestock.

Elsewhere, perhaps because of my lack of knowledge, the evidence is not quite so clear cut, but nevertheless indicates that the greatest sand movement seems to have taken place where sand dunes were in close proximity to medieval settlement. At Rhossili in the Gower the remains of a church and farm have been discovered beneath the dunes, and another church founded in the 12th century, together with a house, are known to lie beneath those at Penmaen.

Closer to home Newton Burrows are associated with a settlement probably founded in the late 1160s. The Merthyr Mawr Warren is similarly associated with an early settlement at Candleston which the dunes later engulfed. Documentary evidence about this area during the medieval period is too scanty to say more, but there was a commercial warren here when John Stradling wrote his Storie of the Lower Burrowes in 1598 (Stradling, 1932). From that document it also seems that at that time livestock from the neighbouring manors of Newton and Tythegston were being pastured here because there was no physical boundary to prevent them wandering from commons in those manors.

In the case of Kenfig the town was founded in the middle years of the 12th century and, as we have seen, livestock and rabbits were introduced to the dunes sometime before 1316.

The valuable research by Leonard Higgins (1933) of Porthcawl and Luke Toft (1988) places the blame for the sand movement in these areas on natural causes, instancing the abnormally high tide levels experienced in Northern Europe caused by the approaching conjunction of the sun and moon in 1433. During the same period planet Earth was entering a period described as a 'climatic low' or, more dramatically, as a 'Mini Ice-Age'. Temperatures fell globally making it impossible to ripen corn on marginal land in upland areas. The most dramatic evidence of this is the extermination of the Viking settlement at Greenland when the population failed to adapt to the changing climate that destroyed their traditional way of farming.

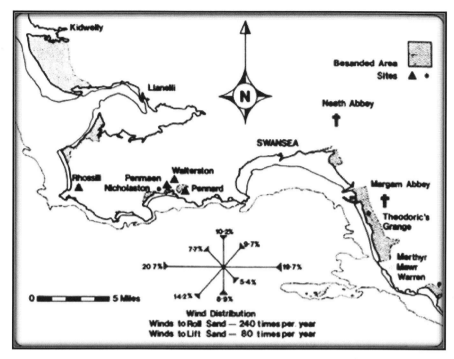

*Map 6: Besanded sites around Swansea Bay (Toft, 1988)*

This change of climate would have been accompanied by deteriorating weather conditions with gales and storms increasing both in number and ferocity. This, according to most scholars, explains why the sand dune areas of South Wales and elsewhere expanded so dramatically during this period. Their line of reasoning is however flawed, for it takes into account only those areas where the dunes did actually advance inland and ignores others where it did not. There are two of these on Swansea Bay, one (as outlined in the main body of this book) being Margam Burrows on the north side of the River Kenfig and the other at Jersey Marine and Crymlyn Burrows between the estuaries of the rivers Neath and Tawe. If the sand movement was due to purely natural causes, then the question as to why these dunes remained as relatively narrow bands immediately inside the foreshore has to be addressed.

In both instances these lands belonged to the monasteries of Margam and Neath respectively. Prior to the abandonment of the town of Kenfig in the first half of the 15th century there is no evidence of any large-scale settlement adjoining Margam Burrows. Although the Abbot obtained a licence to create a rabbit warren here in 1344 it never seems to have been implemented. Similarly there were no villages or lay settlements on the Neath land between the Neath river and Crymlyn brook until comparatively recent times. There were (and probably still are!) rabbits in this area forty years ago, but how long they have been there, and whether they originated with a commercial warren, is not known.

To me the evidence seems perfectly clear. Where dune areas were associated with Norman settlements and/or rabbit warrens during the 12th and 13th centuries they subsequently began moving inland. Where either or both elements were lacking, they did not. From this the conclusion is an obvious one. Removal of the natural vegetation cover through over-grazing left the underlying sand exposed and vulnerable to the forces of nature described by Higgins and Toft. If further evidence were needed, then one only has to look at the state of the Kenfig dunes today.

Livestock grazing gradually dwindled during the early part of the 20th century as the last surviving burgesses (who were the only ones to enjoy common rights here) died out. In the 1950s myxomatosis virtually wiped out the rabbit population which has never really recovered. For half a century therefore little or no grazing took place in the dunes and away from the foreshore these have become overgrown by vegetation and stabilised. Although now covering a far wider area, they have in fact reverted to the state of the inland dunes of the original coastal system that was here at the founding of Kenfig. In such a state the existing vegetation would have been sufficient to quickly reclaim any temporary breaches made by flood and/or gales. It was the presence of grazing livestock, whether cattle, sheep or rabbits, that not only prevented such regeneration, but damaged the overall fabric of plant cover making the dunes vulnerable to the forces of nature.

The best analogy that springs to mind is the little sand castles we made on the beach as children with our buckets and spades. On a dry day a stiff breeze gradually eroded the neat shape created by our upturned buckets, reducing them to shapeless mounds. Any that survived in recognisable form were quickly washed away by the first gentle caress of the incoming tide. Whilst the rising tide levels in the 14th century, and the stormy conditions attributed to the associated 'Mini Ice-Age' **were** a significant factor in the inland march of the sand, they only struck hard at those locations where the fragile eco-systems of the dunes had already been destabilised by over-grazing.

## Postscript (July 2006)

In an attempt to arrest the growth of vegetation across the dunes, the Nature Reserve have recently fenced off a wide area in the north of the reserve to the south of the river so that it can be grazed by cattle as well as sheep. Previous attempts using sheep alone had proved unsuccessful, probably because they are only able to graze very short vegetation. Farmers rearing both sheep and cattle first turn the latter into any new lush pasture and only when they have cropped the grass right down do they replace them with sheep. Hopefully this is what will now happen in the pasture at Kenfig, recreating the conditions that created and maintained the unstable nature of the dunes and thereby protecting the habitat in which the reserve's unique flora and fauna flourishes. Gates have been inserted at various places along the fence boundary to allow public access to the land and the castle ruins within it.

I was also interested to note on a recent visit that a rabbit warren has apparently been established on an area of cleared land just outside the fence and north of Mawdlam. Like sheep, rabbits can only graze short vegetation, and for this reason the colonies of the two surviving warrens in the reserve have apparently been unable to expand into adjoining areas. It will be interesting to see how this experiment progresses in the light of the views I have expressed concerning the origins of the sand movement at Kenfig.

# APPENDIX V

# Dating the Town Ordinances and Charters

### Dating the Ordinances

The heading of the Kenfig Ordinances describes how they had been re-written "word by word and agreeable to the old decayed roule, with other more ordinances added thereunto". This "old decayed roule" was dated to the year 1330, and the copy was probably the one made in the 1740s when Edward Harris was Portreeve of Kenfig as set out in his accounts for that period.

When the Borough of Kenfig first came into being the burgesses would have sent somebody to an existing Borough (probably Cardiff or Neath) to obtain a copy of the bylaws already in force there. These would then have formed the basis for the ones for their new town, perhaps adopted in their entirety or in some cases amended and discarded to conform with their own particular requirements.

These bylaws or 'ordinances' would have been written out in tabular form, one beneath the other, on a sheet of parchment, and continued on subsequent sheets that were then stitched together so they could be rolled up and tied for storage when not in use. When a new ordinance was adopted it was written in after the last entry so that the roll gradually grew in length with the new laws being added in a rough chronological sequence.

Unfortunately the copy of the Kenfig ordinances we possess does not identify at which point the original bylaws terminated and "other more ordinances added". That "old decayed roule" would itself have been copied from a previous document and the change of handwriting would certainly have enabled us to identify those ordinances added subsequent to that date. Perhaps somebody more familiar with such documents might be able to discern this division (and identify the earliest ones implemented at the time of the town's foundation) simply by studying the text of the existing copy. I, alas, possess no such specialist knowledge, but thanks to the good offices of Mr Brian Ll. James of Cardiff (cf. Merrick, 1578), I can suggest the point the Kenfig Ordinances had reached by the year 1254.

Mr James kindly sent me a copy of the Ordinances of the Borough of Cowbridge dating from 1601. What immediately struck me was that 46 out of the first 48 of these were virtually word for word identical with the first 46 from the Kenfig Roll. Almost the only difference was that the chief authority at Cowbridge was a pair of bailiffs, whilst at Kenfig it was the Portreeve. From this it seems reasonable to assume that when the Borough of Cowbridge was created between 1249 and 1254 its burgesses had used Kenfig's Ordinances as a model for their own, virtually adopting them intact, adding two new ones to answer their own particular requirements.

This theory seems to be borne out by Kenfig Ordinance No 46 and its Cowbridge counterpart (also No 46). The sense of both is very similar, but unlike the other 45 identical Ordinances the wording is very different.

| Kenfig Ordinance No 46 | Cowbridge Ordinance No 46 |
|---|---|
| It is ordained that noe burgess or burgesses be admitted to be putt in election for portreeve, nor in the councell of the said town, nor in any other office with the said burrough except he or they be dwellers therein. | Ytt is Ordeyned that noe maner of person be admitted to be Alderman nor Burgesse within the said towne, excepte he be a dweller therein. And yf any of the Aldermen or Burgesses departe from the said Towne and dwell in an other place, him or them to be disomyned that soe departethe. |

It is almost as though the Kenfig burgesses made their Cowbridge counterparts aware of a particular problem they faced at that time, and a new law they intended to bring in to combat it. The Cowbridge burgesses took this on board and subsequently framed their own bylaw along similar lines, but in their own words.

Taken all-in-all, it therefore seems that the first 45 Kenfig Ordinances were in being by 1254 when Cowbidge came into being, and No 46 added about that time. It also seems safe to say that the next four bylaws (Nos 47-50) were added after this date but before the year 1397. This is because by Thomas le Despenser's charter of that year the Kenfig Burgesses were given a new common at Kenfig Down and the right of common at The Rugge (Cefn Cribwr). Ordinance No 50 deals specifically to problems arising from the use of such common land, but only refers to 'our common' in the singular. The next Ordinance also deals with matters relating to common land, but unfortunately not in terms that allow us to infer whether there was one or more. No 52 is dated, and relates to the enclosure of part of the Common on The Rugge in 1572.

From this it is therefore possible to show a certain basic sequence for the Kenfig Ordinances:

| Nos 1 – 45 | Made pre 1254 |
|---|---|
| No 46 | Made circa 1249-1254 |
| Nos 47-50 | Made 1254-1397 |
| No 51 | Made pre 1572 |
| No 52 | Made 1572 (Dated) |
| Nos 53-58 | Made 1572-1773 |
| No 59 | Made 1773 (Dated) |

## Dating the Margam Charters

Most of the charters amongst the Margam Abbey collection that belong to the late 12th and early 13th century are undated which means that their value as historical documents are severely limited. Many years ago therefore (and long before I acquired a computer!) I attempted to assign them at least an approximate date and believe that in this I achieved a certain measure of success.

In the main I relied upon four main methods to assign (as closely as possible) the date to which a particular charter belonged.

### 1. Confirmation Charters.
From time to time the Abbots of Margam secured a confirmation of all grants made to the monastery up to that time from leading lay and ecclesiastical figures. Those from whom such charters were obtained included the Pope, Kings of England, Lords of Glamorgan and Bishops of Llandaff. Some are dated, others are not though in the case of the latter it was often possible to pin them down to within a year or two.

It follows that if property confirmed in one such charter was not mentioned in the one that preceded it, then the document by which it had been conveyed to the Abbey had been issued some time between the two. In one or two instances the length of the period during which such a charter may have been issued is too great to be of any practical value, but the principal ones I used were the following:

| Charter | *Ref* | *Notes on Date* | *Date* |
|---|---|---|---|
| King Henry II | PM 11 | Undated but presumably made when Earl William was imprisoned by the King 1173-1177*. Witnesses confirm 1174-1179. | 1174-7 |
| King Henry II | PM 13 | Ditto | 1174-7 |
| Pope Urban III | Harley Ch 75 A 1 | Dated document | 1186 |
| Pope Innocent III | PM 83 | Dated Document | 1203 |
| King John | PM 289.30 | Dated Document | 1206 |
| King John | PM 98 | Dated Document | 1207 |
| Countess Isabel | PM 113 | Undated. Made by the Countess with assent of her husband the Earl of Essex. They married 1214 and he died two years later. | 1214-6 |
| Countess Isabel | PM 113C | Undated. After the death of the Earl of Essex her husband (1216) but before her own (1217). | 1216-7 |
| Gilbert de Clare | PM 212 B C | Undated & confirmed by an Inspeximus of 1338.He succeeded the Countess who died 1217, but Henry Bishop of Llandaff who was a witness died in 1218. | 1217-8 |

## 2. Officials mentioned in the Charters.

These included not just major personages such as Lords of Glamorgan, Bishops of Llandaff, and the Abbots of Margam, but even minor figures such as the Sheriffs, Priors of the Abbey, and constables of castles (Kenfig in particular). Sometimes there was firm evidence, whether from the charters or elsewhere, that these people held office in a particular year, and it was usually often possible to determine a sequence of holders. Whilst firm dates could not, in most cases, be assigned to the periods certain officer-holders were current, once the sequence had been determined then it was often possible to determine the earliest and latest dates at which he could conceivably have held the post.

---

* Clark, GT, 'Land of Morgan pp 59-60.

As an example, the following is the sequence of Cellarers at Margam either side of the year 1200:

**Roger**. He appears in charters which date no earlier than 1177, and no later than 1189 including one document dated to 1188.

**William**. Occurs in a document dated 1207 and another which cannot be later than 1189 so he evidently succeeded Roger in 1188-9

**Andrew**. Occurs in several undated documents in the early decades of the 13th century, none of which can be earlier than 1207 because William held office at that time. One document in which he appears cannot be later than 1219.

From the above it follows that any document that includes Roger as the Cellarer pre-dates 1189, whilst those in which Andrew is shown post-date 1207. William, who held office during the intervening period between the two cannot have done so earlier than 1188 or later than 1219, and any charters in which he occurs as the Cellarer will belong to that period.

Whilst the gaps in the dating sequences could (as in this instance) be quite large when taken in conjunction with those of other officers listed, the Confirmations Charters, and family sequences (see below), this can often be reduced to date the document within a decade.

**3. Family Sequences.**

These were usually not so helpful as those of the office-holders, but where a definite sequence of family members could be established, then it can be used in the same manner. Sequences for the Lords of Avan, the Lageles family of Laleston, and the De Cornelly family of South Cornelly were fairly straightforward, but others like the Lovels of North Cornelly who used the same Christian name for their eldest son (in their case 'Walter') are more difficult. In the case of the Lovels in fact it is virtually impossible!

## 4. Document Sequences.

In certain cases there are several documents relating to a particular manor or parcel of land, and it is usually a simple matter to arrange these in chronological order. Once approximate dates have been established for one or more charters in the sequence then it is usually possible to assign approximate periods to the others.

Having assigned provisional dates to many of the charters by using this method it was then necessary to review the dates assigned to the individuals in the light of this information. I am currently undertaking a second such review, but since I lack the knowledge and the means to create a computer programme that would assist in this task, then it is still virtually a pencil and paper exercise. Perhaps one day somebody will be able to take this idea forward using computer technology and improve on my rather amateurish efforts which have nevertheless achieved results as the following examples illustrate.

**PM 6. A Grant of land by Abbot Conan to Gregory & Hugh , nephews of Helias the Clerk.** The Abbot himself cannot have held the office earlier than 1175 or later than 1196. John the Prior of Ewenny cannot be earlier than 1180, and Roger the Cellarer at Margam (as indicated above) did not hold that office later than 1189. The charter therefore dates from post 1180, but pre 1189.

**PM 32. Notification by Hugh de Hereford that he has granted all his land to the Abbey.** This final grant is confirmed by Pope Urban's Bull of 1186 which it therefore pre-dates. Neither this, nor any other of the preceding charters by which Hugh gave his land piecemeal to the monks is confirmed by the charters of King Henry II, so it cannot be earlier than 1176. The fact that Hugh made the gift partly for the soul of Earl William of Gloucester who died in 1183 suggests that the document was sealed in the years 1183-1186.

**Harley Charter 75 B 16. Clarification by William de Bonville of a grant to the Abbey by his father John, with the addition of further lands.** John de Bonville was certainly still alive as late as the year 1200, and his grant is not listed in the Bull of Pope Urban (1203).William had been succeeded as lord of Bonvilston by Roger de Bonville by the year 1222 at the very latest, and the witness Herbert de St Quentin cannot be later than 1215. The land given or confirmed by William to the monks totalled 50 acres, which is the amount confirmed as the gifts of the family in the Confirmation Charter of King John (1205). This document therefore was issued in the period between the two confirmations 1203-1205.

**Harley Charter 75 C 24. Riered son of Kenaf granted to the monks a fourth part of the land of Bradington.** Henry of Abergavenny was Bishop of Llandaff 1193-1218, but this charter post-dates Harley Charter 75 A 18 in which this fourth part was quit-claimed to Riered and is dated 1199. Morgan ap Caradoc was Lord of Avan and does not occur after the year 1208. The document therefore belongs to the period 1199-1208.

In all the above cases (which I selected largely at random) it has been possible to pin-point the date of the documents concerned to within a decade or less. This is not unusual, particularly for ones belonging to the period 1176 to 1217 which is covered by Confirmation Charters that are either dated or can be assigned to a very close period of just three years or less.

# APPENDIX VI

## The Angel Inn and the Kenfig Malderia

The Angel Inn at Mawdlam is a popular local hostelry that stands on the NE side of the church of Saint Mary Magdalene and its graveyard. From written records it would appear that in 1731 the licensee was a Kenfig burgess named Hopkin Thomas (1671-1743) who was twice reported for selling ale "less than measure" in that year. This, to date, is the earliest indication I have found for the existence of an inn or alehouse at this location. The early map of Kenfig drawn by Thomas Wyseman in 1592 was intended to illustrate a dispute relating to the boundaries of the common on Kenfig Down, and beyond its boundaries cannot be relied upon as it contains several inaccuracies. His depiction of the village of Mawdlam (then known as Kenfig) does nevertheless appear to indicate two houses east of the church. These are set back from the main settlement either side of Heol Las, and may be intended to represent The Angel Inn and the farm house called Ty'n y Towyn which both lay in this area.

In the 1940s the premises were still much the same as they probably were in Hopkin's day – a long low rectangular building with a thatched roof that was peculiar in that the main entrance was set in the side furthest away from the road. My own feeling is that during the medieval period this road ran much further to the north (see below), nevertheless this still means that the building was rather inconveniently placed in relation to the other medieval road (Heol Las) which passed along the south side of the church and still forms the main street of the village.

In 1953/4 the brewery that owned the property carried out major structural alterations – including the creation of an entrance at what is now the front of the building. As part of this alteration an extension was created on the south side of the pub so that the external wall visible in the photographs is now an internal wall and any surviving features upon it (such as blocked up windows and doors) covered by rendering and bar fittings.

About two years ago I became aware of the possibility that the inn, together with the church (first mentioned in a document of circa 1255), may have been enclosed within a walled compound (of which the present churchyard was only a part) as elements of a medieval hospital or 'malederia'.

That there was such a 'malederia' or 'hospital' near the town of Kenfig is known from a reference to it in a manuscript (PM 79) in the Penrice & Margam collection at the National Library of Wales. The relevant text (Birch, 1897: 65) reads:

[Grant by Richard of Dunster] with counsel and consent of his wife and heirs, of his burgage in Kenefeg, with land adjoining the castle of the same town, and one acre outside the town, near the Malederia

The deed is undated, but the array of witnesses is identical to that in a lease by Roger Grammus (Harley Charter 75 C.3 – Birch p.184) to part of his land between the river Kenfig and the Goylake (Avan Fach) which commenced at Christmas 1202.

Dunster's grant tells us only that the malederia lay outside the town which, in the context of the period could also mean the boundary of the borough and, as we now realise, the medieval Borough of Kenfig was far smaller than the one abolished in 1886.

On the south the medieval boundary was the road running from Taddlecross (Croes y Ddadl) to "the cross", which course is followed by the present road from Mawdlam to Pyle though arguably slightly further south than the original due to sand encroachment. Mawdlam church and The Angel Inn therefore lay just outside the town or borough boundary as the Dunster charter indicates, and were also adjacent to what was apparently the main road into the town from Cardiff (Heol Las). This would tend to be the case with such a hospital especially if, as Birch suggests, it was a leper house. One of the main purposes of these establishments was to prevent lepers or the sick lingering in the town and spreading their contagion amongst the inhabitants.

Locally it has always been maintained that The Angel was originally an inn for pilgrims making their way to St David's. So difficult was this journey that two pilgrimages here were considered equal to one made to the holiest shrine in Christendom at Jerusalem. Our local legend may therefore contain an element of truth, for at the time the malederia was in being, leprosy and other illnesses were regarded as God's punishment inflicted upon an individual for some sin he or she had committed. Consequently the main element in any cure involved a displays of piety and contrition so going on a pilgrimage was a popular method of accomplishing this. The identity of the benefactor who took pity on their plight by building them hospital accommodation at Kenfig is unknown,

The realisation that Mawdlam church may well be the location of the hospital came to me whilst watching a *Time Team* excavation on the site of a leper house near Winchester. Like Mawdlam it was situated just outside the town boundary, but well away from the actual town itself. The local archaeologist stated that one of the reasons for believing that the empty field to which he had directed the team was the site of these premises was that a chapel dedicated to Saint Mary Magdalene had formerly stood there. He then added that chapels with such a dedication were almost invariably associated in medieval times with leper houses or hospitals.

Over the three days of their dig the team uncovered evidence of all the elements associated with a medieval leper house in what was claimed to be the most comprehensive investigation of such an establishment to date. The accommodation provided for the lepers was in the form of a long, oblong building divided internally into several rooms, each with its own entrance facing towards the chapel. It was explained that each would have housed one leper and possibly their family travelling with them.

This building (which had later been converted into almshouses) was roughly parallel to the chapel, and at right angles between them was another building which was identified as the house of the master in charge of the establishment. The other feature excavated was part of the cemetery, and it was confirmed that the

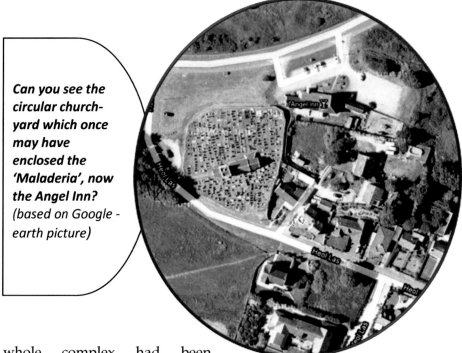

*Can you see the circular church-yard which once may have enclosed the 'Maladeria', now the Angel Inn?* (based on Google - earth picture)

whole complex had been enclosed within a boundary wall.

Although outside the wall of the present churchyard, The Angel at Mawdlam stands in similar relationship to the church. Furthermore, as previously stated, prior to alterations made to the premises in the 1950s its main entrance was on the side facing away from the main road and towards the chapel. In fact, there was formerly no access whatsoever to the building on the north side adjoining the road, and it was locally referred to as 'the back-to-front inn'.

If the chapel were not attached to a leper house, then one would expect it to be part of a village community, and despite several other suggestive features this does not seem to have been the case. On the one hand the evidence for an early settlement at Mawdlam is quite persuasive in that clearly the land here was under cultivation during the period of the old town. On old maps the remnants of former strip fields is quite evident. Documents from the 17th and 18th centuries likewise indicate that enclosures such as Winters Hill, Winters Mead and Brombil Mawr were former common fields that still contained some individual plots owned by certain individuals. An undated medieval charter (PM 2013) records the gift by Robert Norrensis to Margam Abbey of an acre of land at Kenfig near a stream that separated his land from that of 'Pishulle'. Pishill or Paschal Hill is the ridge running south from Mawdlam church towards Kenfig Down, where former field patterns seem to indicate medieval cultivation.

It would be natural to assume that such cultivation would have stemmed from the inhabitants of a neighbouring village, but it might equally have been undertaken by Kenfig burgesses who were granted land in the immediate vicinity of the church under their charter of 1397.

There is indeed no documentary evidence mentioning a settlement here. The earliest reference to the chapel actually suggests that none existed as it describes Heol Las as the road leading to the chapel of Saint Mary Magdalene (Birch, 1897: 152-3) — not to a named community that it may have been designed to serve. If there was no such community, then the chapel must have served some other purpose. The same criteria applies to the grant of land to the burgesses by Thomas le Despenser in his charter of 1397 — it is described in relationship to the chapel, not any community.

A feature of the little church today is the magnificently carved font, but both because of its size and its quality I would not be the first to suggest that it was not original. The favoured explanation is that it was rescued from the abandoned church of Saint James of Kenfig, which in turn begs the question as to why it never went to the one at Pyle with the rest of the demolition material. Did the burgesses perhaps just help themselves to it without asking, or were they perhaps allowed to have it because there was no font at Mawdlam as would perhaps have been the case if it had not been built to serve the needs of a village community?

Finally, there are indications that at the time Kenfig town was abandoned the chapel at Mawdlam itself was a ruin, which would be unthinkable if it were serving an existing village. Yet two writers during the Tudor period state that Mawdlam church was built by the burgesses after they had evacuated the town. According to Rice Merrick (1578) "the church was newly builded upon the hill". In 1592 Thomas Wyseman in his report on a boundary dispute with Sker (PM MS 9616) also claims that the village was built at the same time—"the bugesses hath been dryven of late tyme to buylde them selfes manny new dwellyngs and a new churche further from the sea (and?) sande towards the lande".

If there was an earlier village at Mawdlam then it seems odd that its church should have been allowed to fall into ruin. If there was not, then an explanation is needed for its construction at this location, pointing again to the possibility that it originally formed an element in the 'malederia'.

Finally, there is the shape of the churchyard that surrounds the chapel of Saint Mary Magdalene. On the north, south and west it describes an irregular oval around the main building, but on the east the wall is straight giving it the appearance that it is later and perhaps erected to cut off that end of an original oval enclosure. Just beyond this wall is a large private house that was originally 'The Butchers Arms', and before that a farmhouse called Ty'n y Towyn which (in the 18th century) was part of a freeholding that included The Angel Inn.

Access to this former farmhouse was, and is, via a short length of track off Heol Las. The configuration of the churchyard wall and this building may therefore indicate that originally the enclosure extended further east, with a building that later became the farmhouse included within it.

I am not qualified enough even to hazard a guess at the age of the architecture apparent at the inn today, and so far as I can ascertain, nobody else has attempted to do so either. All that can be said is that the thickness of the walls suggest it is very old, but as indicated above, if it existed in the 13th century then its location is peculiar. It adjoined neither the Taddulcrosse road (which was at the back of the building where there was apparently no door) nor Heol Las, but this isolation might be explained if it was indeed the accommodation at the malederia and was originally enclosed with the church within a boundary wall.

The most convincing piece of evidence regarding the original use of this building, however, recently came to hand in the form of copies of three photographs sent to me by Mr John Lyons of Narberth.(Apologies for the poor quality) Nos 1 & 2 seem to date from the early years of the 20th century, and the third from the 1940s. What John actually sent are greatly enlarged photocopies of the originals which I have reduced and reproduced with these notes. The limitations of my computer and the reduction in size means that not all the features apparent on my copies and mentioned in the text below are as clear on these images.

No 1 shows the 'front' of the inn facing towards the church and has been taken from the South-east. Furthest from the camera is what appears to be an extension to the original building. At the pine end of this is the 'Flemish chimney' apparent today. The main building has four upstairs widows over which the eves of the thatched roof is carried in a 'festoon' style. Interestingly it is also lifted over a 'blind' spot just to the right of the main door which seems to imply that a fifth window formerly existed at that point.

*Photograph No 1*

*Photograph No 2*

The two upstairs widows nearest the viewer are matched by ground floor widows immediately below. Photograph No 2 seems to indicate that both of these (particularly the one nearest the main entrance) are set into larger blocked up apertures. In the case of the latter the outline appears to include that of the upper part of a doorway.

**Photograph No 3**

*In the picture: Barbara Morgan and on the right, A Leslie Evans*

Returning to photograph No 1, below the 'blind spot' the indications of another blocked-up doorway are faintly visible (though not so clear on my computer copy) and more clearly in photograph No 2. The straight edge of one side of this door can also be made out to the right of the group of people in photograph No 3. In No2 the outlines of a former step is apparent set at an angle to the slope of the base of the wall, and there are indications of a similar step beneath the widow on its right.

Below the next upstairs window (on the left of the 'blind spot') is the main entrance to the public house with the sign giving the name of the premises and the details of the licensee above. The next ground floor window on the west is larger than all the others in this part of the building suggesting it is a later insertion.

Immediately below the furthest upstairs window the wall of the building is blank, and the next widow on the ground floor is set somewhat to the left or west. This becomes more apparent in photograph No 2, where it is clear that another blocked-up doorway exists below the upstairs window – the former lintel being particularly prominent in my copy. The outline of this doorway is again faintly visible in picture No. 3.

At the furthest end of the building there is an existing door, though here there is no upstairs window, nor are the eaves of the thatch 'lifted', but there may have been one here originally. These photographs therefore seem to show that at one time there existed at least five doors on this side of the building, four of them associated with a window immediately above. On this basis it seems likely that the ground floor window at the eastern end of the building also marks the site of a former doorway, and that the doorway at the western end perhaps originally had a window above.

It therefore appears possible that originally the main building was indeed divided up into five or six separate dwellings, each with its own entrance, and identical to the leper accommodation uncovered in the Time Team excavation. These could, in truth, be almshouses (though there is no record of the latter ever having existed in the area), but taken together with the other evidence I have outlined, I believe it highly likely that, with the church, it formed part of the original malederia.The extension with the 'Flemish chimney' at the western end may be a later addition, but on the other hand it could be the former 'master's house' of the original establishment. If I am right, then we have here at Mawdlam a quite remarkable survival from the days of the medieval town of Kenfig.

# REFERENCES:

**Ailesbury, Marquis of** (1962) *A History of Savernake Forest* Devizes: Charles Woodward

*Annals of Margam* *1066-1232* Annales Monastici: 1 36 Rolls Series H. R. Luard (ed.) London 1864 (repr. 1965))

**Appleby, John T** (1969) *The Troubled Reign of King Stephen*; London, Bell & Sons.

**Birch, Walter De Gray** (1897) *A history of Margam Abbey : derived from the original documents in the British Museum, H.M. Record Office, the Margam muniments, etc* London, Bedford Press.    Available at http://openlibrary.org/books/OL7235581M/A_history_of_Margam_Abbey

**Butler, Lawrence** (2005) Dolforwyn Castle, *Current Archaeology* No 197, 296-234

**Carr, A P** (1975) *Swansea Bay (Sker) Project, Progress report for the period to March 1975 and subsequent developments.* Institute of Oceanographic Sciences, Report 20; available from: *www.soton.ac.uk/library/about/nol/iosiosdlreportslist.doc.* See also Reports Nos. 26, 42, 48, 51, 60, 74, 92, 93, 98, 99, 105 and 118 from the same source

**Cherry, John** (1991)*'Leather'* – *English Medieval Industries;* Blair & Ramsay (eds); Hambledon & London

**Clark, G T** (1880) The Land of Morgan: its conquest and its conquerors. Being a contribution towards the history of Glamorgan. *Journal of the Royal Archæological Institute.* London, Whiting & Co

**Clark, George Thomas** (1910) *Cartae et Alia Munimenta quae ad Dominium de Glamorgan pertinent* 6 vols. Cardiff, William Lewis

**Cowley, F G** (1977) *The Monastic Order in South Wales, 1066-1349;* Cardiff: University of Wales Press.

**Crouch, David** (1991) The Last Adventure of Richard Siward, *Morgannwg* Vol XXXV

**Davies, J R** (2003) *The Book of Llandaf and the Norman Church in Wales,* Woodbridge UK, Boydell Press

**Donovan, Edward** (1805) *Descriptive Excursions through South Wales and Monmouthshire in the Year 1804, and the Four Preceding Summers* Vol 2 London: Rivingtons.

**Evans, A Leslie** (1964) *The Story of Kenfig;* Port Talbot

**Evans, A Leslie** (n/k) *Leyson D'Avene* unpub MSS

**Evans, Frederic** (1912) *"Tir Iarll." The Earl's Land, comprising the ancient parishes of Llangynwyd, Bettws, Margam, and Kenfig* [Welsh "County" Series] Cardiff, Educational Publishing Co. Reprinted & pub by Mid Glamorgan Co Library 1993

**Giraldus Cambrensis** (Gerald of Wales). (1987) *The Journey through Wales / The Description of Wales;* trans. by Lewis Thorpe; London: Penguin Classics

**Gillham, Mary** (1987) *Sand Dunes (Glamorgan Heritage Coast Wildlife Series Volume 1).* Glamorgan Wildlife Trust: Bridgend

**Gray, Thomas** (1909) *The Buried City of Kenfig;* London, T Fisher Unwin;

**Griffiths, Barrie** (1990) *Sturmi's Land*  Unpublished MSS available at Bridgend County Libraries.

**Griffiths, Barrie** (1996-1998) *Medieval Kenfig,* Parts I – V; The Kenfig Society

**Griffiths, Barrie** (2002) *The Five Mills of Kenfig;* The Kenfig Society

**Griffiths, B & Lyons, J** (1996) *Llyfnwy's History of Kenfig;* The Kenfig Society

***Gwenllian Brut*** "a chronicle now known to be a forgery" HC Harley MSS at the British Museum

**Higgins, L. S**. (1933) An Investigation into the Problem of the Sand Dune Area of the South Wales Coast; *Archaeologia Cambrensis* Vol LXXXVIII

**Hopkins, Anthony** (1988) *Medieval Neath;* Nidum Publications

**Jones, Peter Simpson** (1993) *Ecological and hydrological studies of dune slack vegetation at Kenfig National Nature Reserve, Mid Glamorgan.* Thesis (Ph.D.) - Cardiff 1993. Pure and Applied Biology

**Leland, John** (1549) *The laboryouse journey  serche of Johan Leylande, for Englandes antiquitees, geven of hym as a newe yeares gyfte to kynge Henry the viij. in the xxxvij. yeare of his reygne, with declaracyons enlarged: by Johan Bale. B.L* London: John Bale

**Luard H R** (1864) *Annals of Margam 1066-1232* Annales Monastici: 1 36 Rolls Series H. R. Luard (ed.) London 1864

**Merrick, Rice** (1578) *Morganiae Archaiographia (A Booke of Glamorganshire's Antiquities),* Re-published 1983 by The South Wales Record Society, Barry Island (Brian Ll. James ed.)

**North, F J** (1957) *Sunken Cities. Some legends of the coast and lakes of Wales* Cardiff: University of Wales Press

**Ordnance Survey** & Index re survey of Local area for Historical Sites at Bridgend Co Library

**Painter, Sidney** (1966) *The Reign of King John*; Baltiore US, Johns Hopkins UP

**PM, Penrice & Margam MSS** – National Library of Wales, Aberystwyth.

**Randall, H J** (1961) *The Vale of Glamorgan*; *Studies in Landscape and History* Newport, R H Johns Ltd

**Randall, H J** (1953) *Bridgend – The Story of a Market Town* Newport, R H Johns Ltd Mid Glamorgan County Library Service reprint 1994.

**RCAHMW (**Royal Commission on Historical & Ancient Monuments Wales)(1991) *Inventory of Ancient Monuments in Glamorgan, Vol III, Part 1a, The Early Castles,* HMSO

**RCAHMW**, (Royal Commission on Historical & Ancient Monuments Wales) (1982) *Volume III, Part II, Medieval Non-defensive Secular Monuments*

**Richard, A J** (1927) Kenfig Castle, *Arch. Camb.* 161-182

**Robbins, Terry** (2002) *Digging up Kenfig*; The Kenfig Society

**Smith, J Beverly** (1958) The Lordship of Glamorgan, *Morgannwg* Vol II,

**Soulsby, I** (1983) *The Towns of Medieval Wales,* Chichester, Phillimore,

**Stradling, John** (1932) *The Storie of the Lower Borowes of Merthyrmawr . ed. Henry John Randall & William Rees* Cardiff: South Wales and Monmouth Record Society. Pub. no. 1.

**Toft, L A** (1988) A Study of CoastalVillage Abandonment in the Swansea Bay Region 1270-1540; *Morgannwg* Vol XXXII

# INDEX

*KENFIG FOLK 2:*

## The BOROUGH In THE SANDS

### The Story of Kenfig and its People 1485-1699

This will continue the story of the Borough into the Tudor Period and onwards to the year 1699. Here Barrie Griffiths looks at its history through the eyes of the people who lived there, and to follows the lives of certain individuals and families to whom Kenfig was 'home'. We also follow their battle to keep the Borough organisation in being, and to amend and adapt its institutions to meet the altered circumstances of its situation. Their battle against the sand encroachment that had claimed their medieval town and castle was far from over, and more fields, buildings, and even a small hamlet were lost during these years. Then there were the religious changes spawned by Henry VIII's break with Rome which split our tiny community to its core with rival groups of Catholics, Nonconformists and Anglicans. Amongst all this upheaval and change, a living still had to be made and children fed.

Available in later in 2011, or early 2012.

Parts 3, 4 and 5 will be published (subject to sufficient demand for the earlier books) annually after that. Eventually, perhaps a 'complete boxed set' will be produced — a fitting memorial to Barrie Griffiths, who was a diligent historian who both illuminated and entertained.

# Over the years the Kenfig Society has published many booklets on the History and People of Kenfig:

| | | | |
|---|---|---|---|
| 1 | 1991 | Kenfig Society | The ancient Borough of Kenfig |
| 2 | 1992 | O.C. Trinder | Sketches of old Kenfig & district |
| 3 | 1993 | Barrie Griffiths | Crimes of the Kenfig district 1740-1840 |
| 4 | 1994 | Barrie Griffiths | A Chronicle of Kenfig Borough |
| 5 | 1994 | *Yvonne Carr* | *Shipwrecks around and about Kenfig (available as a re-print)* |
| 6 | 1995 | Barrie Griffiths | Folktales of Pyle and Kenfig |
| 7 | 1996 | Barrie Griffiths | Kenfig's Portreeves 1659 - 1775 Some important people from Kenfig's past |
| 8 | 1996 | John Lyons&BG | Llyfnwy's History of Kenfig 1857 |
| 9 | 1996 | Barrie Griffiths | Medieval Kenfig Part I: The Founding |
| 10 | 1997 | Barrie Griffiths | Kenfig As Others Saw It Visitors Accounts of Kenfig 1530 - 1930 |
| 11 | 1997 | Dennis Jones | What the papers said 1866-69 (vol1) |
| 12 | 1997 | Barrie Griffiths | Medieval Kenfig Part II: The Frontier Town |
| 13 | 1997 | Barrie Griffiths | Medieval Kenfig Part III: A Town for Merchandise |
| 14 | 1998 | Dennis Jones | What the papers said Vol 2 1870-72 |
| 15 | 1998 | Dennis Jones | What the papers said Vol 3 1873-74 |
| 16 | 1998 | Barrie Griffiths | Medieval Kenfig Part IV: Town and Castle |
| 17 | 1998 | Barrie Griffiths | Medieval Kenfig Part V, "ruined and choked by the sand". |
| 18 | 1999 | Barrie Griffiths | Tales of Our Century Pt I: 1900-44 |
| 19 | 1999 | Barrie Griffiths | Tales of Our Century Pt I: 1949-99 |

| | | | |
|---|---|---|---|
| *20* | *1999* | *Barrie Griffiths* | *A Spy for Wellington*<br>*Sir John William Waters 1774 - 1842.*<br>*(available as a re-print)* |
| **21** | **2000** | **Barrie Griffiths** | **The House at Sker Point (1e)  2002 (2e)** |
| 22 | 2001 | Dennis Jones | What the papers said Vol 4 1875-76 |
| *23* | *2001* | *Barrie Griffiths* | *The Inn at Pyle (available as a re-print)* |
| 24 | 2001 | Dennis Jones | What the papers said Vol 5 1877-78 |
| 25 | 2002 | Barrie Griffiths | The Five mills of Kenfig |
| **26** | **2002** | **Barrie Griffiths** | **Welcome to Kenfig** (in print) |
| 27 | 2002 | Dennis Jones | What the papers said Vol 6 1890-80 |
| **28** | **2002** | **Terry Robbins** | **Digging Up Kenfig** (in print) |
| **29** | **2004** | **Dennis Jones** | **What the papers said Vol 7 Jan-Dec 1881** |
| **30** | **2005** | **Barrie Griffiths** | **Once Upon a Time in Kenfig**  (in print) |
| **31** | **2005** | **Dennis Jones** | **What the paper's said Vol 8 Jan-Dec 1882** (in print) |
| **32** | **2007** | **BG & CJ** | **Time Trekker** (in print) |
| 33 | 2008 | *John Blundell* | *From Kenfig to Ogmore:*<br>*A personal history of the coast*<br>*(available as a re-print)* |

Titles which are currently available are shown in **bold** on this list. Some re-prints are available which are shown *in italics*, but check with our website — we are still adding titles to our re-print list.

For more details log on to our website:

# www.kenfigsociety.org